101 CREATIVE TOUCHES

Published by BBC Books
BBC Worldwide Ltd, Woodlands,
80 Wood Lane, London W12 0TT

First published for
Marks & Spencer in 2003
This edition published in 2005
Copyright © BBC Worldwide 2003
All photographs © *BBC Good Homes*
magazine 2003. Please see page 223 for
a list of the contributors.

ISBN 0 563 52255 0

Edited by Alison Willmott
Commissioning Editor: Vivien Bowler
Project Editor: Julia Charles
Series Design: Claire Wood
Book Design: Kathryn Gammon
Design Manager: Annette Peppis
Production Controller: Christopher Tinker

Set in Amasis MT and ITC Officina Sans
Printed and bound in Italy by LEGO SpA
Colour origination by Butler & Tanner

101 CREATIVE TOUCHES

STYLISH HOME IDEAS

Julie Savill

Good Homes

CONTENTS

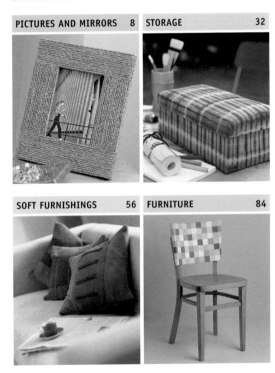

INTRODUCTION

How often have you finished decorating a room only to think that it doesn't look quite right, that somehow something is missing? Once the fresh paint is on the walls, the new blinds are at the windows and the furniture is in place there's still one more step to go before your room makeover is complete. That final stage is to put your personality and individuality into the room and it's where this book earns its keep. *101 Creative Touches* is crammed full of all the little ideas that put the designer seal on a room and it's these tiny touches that will bring any scheme to life and make it completely your own.

At *BBC Good Homes* magazine we believe these little design tricks should be quick to create (an hour is about the most many of us can spare to make something), affordable (why make it if you could buy it ready-made for less) and full of impact. We have built up a wealth of clever projects that fulfil these criteria and they are all here in *101 Creative Touches* ready for you to use to add an individual note to your home. None of them need any specialist skills and anyone who has an urge to get creative will be able to tackle all of the projects found here.

One word I would add here is to anyone who thinks they can't sew. Do yourself a favour and give it a go. A simple sewing machine is a small investment that will pay for itself time and time again. Even if you only feel confident stitching a straight line it will mean you can make your own cushion covers, blinds, simple curtains and bed throws saving you hundreds and hundreds of pounds and giving you access to unlimited looks for your home. Get into sewing and suddenly the remnant fabric bin at your local department store becomes a treasure chest that you won't be able to pass by. Most department stores have demonstration areas where you can test different machines, ask questions and get advice. Go on, surprise yourself and try it!

Stylists who work on magazines and television makeover programmes know all about the importance of the finishing touches and they have all developed signature tricks of the trade which they can keep reinventing and using again and again to draw a scheme together and make it look truly complete. At *BBC Good Homes* magazine we've been lucky enough to work with some of the very best stylists who are just brimming with ideas for finishing touches. Our special thanks go to Kitty Percy, Alison Jenkins, Juliet Bawden and Petra Boase. I would also like to mention Sophie Robinson, *BBC Good Homes* magazine's talented home editor and her equally skilful predecessor, Wendy Uren, who have both contributed ideas to this book but have also commissioned and overseen the creation of virtually all of the projects here – my thanks to you both.

Julie Savill, Editor
BBC Good Homes magazine

Modern mosaic

The Romans had them down to a fine art, but modern-day mosaics take on simpler, more geometric designs. Follow these steps to make the chic grey-framed mirror. The smaller design is even easier to make as it uses mirror tiles, which need no grouting.

1 Take a 312mm square of 2cm-thick MDF, and seal with a mix of half PVA adhesive, half water. Leave to dry. Using a scalpel, cut borders two tiles wide from sheets of 4mm-thick glass mosaics in dark and pale grey. The outer edges of the larger border should measure 320mm, so they overhang the MDF by 4mm. Apply PVA adhesive to the tiled side of this border, position on the MDF, then repeat for the inner border. Leave to dry.

2 Cut mosaic strips one tile wide for the mirror edges. Squeeze PVA onto the tiled side and press in place so they line up with the border tiles. Leave until the glue is dry.

3 To remove backing paper, dampen with a sponge and leave for several minutes. If it does not peel off easily, dampen again. Stick a 149 × 149mm piece of 4mm-thick mirror to the MDF using PVA and leave to dry.

4 Mix the white grout following the maker's instructions. Using a rubber squeegee, work it into the mosaic to fill the cracks. Repeat along the sides, remove excess with a damp sponge and leave to dry for two days. Wipe clean using a nylon scourer and household cleaning fluid.

TIP
If, after removing the backing paper, you find that PVA has seeped between the tiles, remove it using the scalpel. Secure any loose tiles using superglue.

Natural framework

A touch of natural texture is just what's needed to add interest to cool, contemporary interiors, and this seagrass-covered picture frame is smart enough to blend in beautifully. Seagrass varies in colour and thickness, so it gives an irregular finish that adds to the natural charm. Choose a frame that has a wide border with a plain, smooth surface.

1 Cut strands of seagrass to fit the borders of your frame. The strands to go along the top and bottom parts of the border should be long enough to pass right across the frame and over the edges, so that their ends are concealed at the back. The strands to cover the vertical sides should be cut to finish level with the top and bottom edges of the picture. Before gluing them down, lay all the strands in place on the frame to check that you have cut enough.

2 Cover the frame with impact adhesive, choosing a glue that remains tacky for a while before drying. Starting with the vertical strands, and working from the inside of the border to the edges, carefully stick each length of seagrass in place. Make sure that the ends of the vertical strands line up exactly. Glue down the ends of the horizontal strands at the back of the frame. Leave to dry.

3 To finish, seal your work by brushing the surface of the seagrass with a solution of half PVA adhesive and half water.

TIP
If you want a slightly different look, try covering a frame with other cords or twines, or even chunky knitting wool.

All the best circles

A lively design of squares and circles turns a boring wooden picture frame into an eye-catching contemporary accessory. Cut from paper, the shapes are simply glued in place. The choice of colours is up to you – here soft yellows in closely toning shades complement the mellow honey-coloured wood of the frame. It's best to use thin paper, unless you want a slightly raised effect.

1 Take a plain wooden picture frame with a smooth border and measure the sides to work out how wide the strips of paper need to be. Remove the backing from the frame.

2 Using sharp scissors, cut strips the same width from paper in two or three shades of the same colour, making them long enough to wrap around the sides and inner edges of the frame. Glue in place using PVA adhesive and leave to dry.

3 Cut circles in two different sizes from the same papers, drawing around a coin or bottle top to get the shape. Stick a larger circle of a contrasting shade in the centre of some of the squares, including the uncovered wooden ones. When the glue is dry, stick a smaller circle of another shade inside some of the circles.

4 When dry, give the frame a protective finish by covering it with several coats of clear polyurethane spray varnish, allowing each coat to dry before applying the next.

TIP
If the PVA adhesive seems thick, dilute it by stirring in a small amount of water.

Sea view

Show off a seashore find and a favourite photograph at the same time by turning a piece of rugged driftwood into an unusual picture holder. Driftwood comes in many shapes and sizes, but for this project you will need a reasonably straight piece that hasn't gone too soft. The picture frame is made from two pieces of glass – ask your glass merchant to grind the edges so that they are safe to handle.

1 Use a fret saw to cut a 6mm-wide slot in a piece of driftwood. To do this, drill a hole, feed the saw blade through, attach it to the saw and then start sawing.

2 Sandwich your photo between the two sheets of glass and push them into the slot. You may need to slip a strip of square dowel into the slot first, to make a ledge for the glass to stand on.

TIP
Before taking items from a beach, check that it is not a special conservation site. Never remove anything from the 'strand line' of debris at high water mark, which is home to insects and plant life.

Behind the scenes

Clip frames are among the cheapest types you can buy, but it takes just seconds to give them an individual look. All you need is a favourite piece of fabric to form a backdrop for your chosen photo. Look for one that will complement your room scheme – here a snippet of crisp navy and white ticking sits well among the cool blues of a contemporary interior. Fabrics offer a vast choice of designs and colours, but use your imagination and you're bound to come up with many other materials that will also look good. Examples might include textured handmade papers in different colours, tin foil or wallpaper samples.

1 Cut a piece of fabric exactly the same size as the clip frame. Glue your photo in position on the right side of the fabric or, if you like to swap your pictures around frequently, use Blu-Tack to hold it in place.

2 Take the frame apart, slip the fabric and photo inside, then clip the frame back together – couldn't be simpler!

Shine on

A touch of gold or silver can have a magical effect on uninspiring accessories, transforming them into glamorous features. This mirror frame is embellished with silver gilt cream, which shines against a background of powdery blue. The silver is applied to raised squares created using a simple relief stencilling technique.

1 Paint a plain wooden mirror frame with a base coat of pale blue emulsion and leave to dry. To make a stencil, mark evenly spaced squares on a strip of stencil card or acetate (don't use paper as this will collect moisture and become soggy). Cut out the squares to make a stencil.

2 Place the stencil in position on the frame. Apply white artist's oil or acrylic paint thickly to each of the square cutouts using a metal spatula or an old credit card. Spoon a dollop of paint onto the edge of the card or spatula, and then pull it over the stencil, making sure that all cut areas are filled. Carefully peel away the stencil, without disturbing the raised surface you've created. Repeat until you have stencilled squares all the way down both vertical sides of the frame.

3 When the paint is dry, rub gilt cream over each of the raised squares using a small round brush or your finger.

Piece plan

A classic-style picture goes totally modern if you hang it in a brand-new way, so create a novel wall decoration by pulling your print to pieces and mounting each section on a separate foamboard block. If you don't have a print big enough, you can get a smaller one enlarged at a photocopy shop. You can also ask the shop to customize your image – this one, originally in black and white, has been photocopied in a sepia tone.

1 Using a fine pencil, divide your print into equal squares. Decide on the size of the finished picture and work out how large each square needs to be. Take the print to a photocopy shop and ask them to enlarge each of the squares to the required size. Have the squares laminated – photocopy shops often offer this service.

2 Cut the laminated squares to size, then cut pieces of foamboard to match. Mount the laminated squares on the blocks by gluing them securely in place. Make light pencil marks on the wall to show where each block should be positioned, measuring carefully to space them evenly and ensure that the lines are straight. Attach them to the wall using sticky foam pads or adhesive Velcro.

Bar code art

Everyday images can look quite dramatic when enlarged, and these quirky bar code pictures would make bold decorations for a blank wall. They are created by enlarging a standard bar code on a photocopier, then using the result to make a stencil. As cutting out the lines and numbers for the stencil may take some time, why not use it more than once? Producing a series of identical pictures in different colours and hanging them together will double the impact.

1 Cut a bar code off an empty packet and enlarge it on a photocopier, or ask a copy shop to do this for you. Apply a thin mist of spray adhesive to the copy and stick it to stencil material. Some stencil materials can be cut out using a heat pen, which makes the process quicker, but if you don't want to buy a heat pen use stencil card and do the cutting with a craft knife. Before you start, tape the stencil to a wooden board so that you don't damage your work surface. Cut carefully around each of the lines and numbers.

2 Mix gouache or stencil paint to a thick, creamy consistency. Fix the stencil to a stretched canvas using masking tape and apply the paint with a stencil brush, using a quick dabbing motion. Wash the stencil and brush before going on to your next colour.

Etched effect

Who would guess that this designer-style decoration for a mirror has been created using a spray can? The intricate art of etching, or rather something that looks convincingly like it, can be achieved in minutes using a can of etching spray, which is available from DIY stores and craft shops. With the centre of the mirror masked off, and flower and leaf shapes pasted onto the rest, the spray reaches only the parts you want it to, resulting in this elegant border.

1 Take a plain mirror with a bevelled edge and decide how wide you want the border to be. To mask off the central area, cut a sheet of paper to cover it and stick in position on the glass using spray adhesive. Cover the bevelled edges using masking tape.

2 Cut leaf and flower shapes from paper and stick them to the border in a random pattern, again using spray adhesive.

3 Lay the mirror on newspaper. Apply a thin coat of etching spray and leave to dry, then repeat. When the second coat is dry, carefully remove the masking tape and paper shapes.

Bed of roses

A small picture set against a beautiful backing often looks more stunning than an image that fills the entire frame. Rose petals make a fitting backing for this tiny flower picture, adding an air of luxury and rich colour to its display in a simple wooden frame. Fresh petals have a strong colour but only a short shelf life. If you want a display that will last, press the petals between sheets of blotting paper sandwiched between heavy books for one to three weeks.

1 If you are using fresh petals, press them for an hour or two between greaseproof paper to flatten them. Cut a piece of card the same size as your picture frame and cover with spray adhesive. Arrange the petals on the card, overlapping them to avoid gaps.

2 Spray a little adhesive onto the back of a small photograph or picture. Position it in the centre of the petals and press in place. Insert the card into the frame.

Mat finish

Creativity isn't only about being a skilled artist or craftsman; it can also mean using items in new and exciting ways. Look around your home and you'll probably find lots of things that can be grouped together on a wall to make a novel display. Melamine place mats emblazoned with photographic images are far too eye-catching to do no more than take spills on a table, so use some to brighten up a dull corner. Printed mouse mats offer a similar ready-to-go art solution.

1 Choosing designs that will complement the colour of your wall, gather together a collection of melamine place mats and coasters. Lay them out on the floor first to decide how you want to arrange them.

2 When you have an arrangement you are happy with, fix each mat to the wall using poster strips, available from stationery shops.

TIP
You could also try the group treatment with plates, decorative ceramic tiles, postcards or fancy picture frames.

Snap happy

Slot your holiday snaps or family photos into this home-made album, which opens out concertina fashion to create an instant gallery along a shelf or mantelpiece. Easy to make from cardboard, with patterned paper or fabric to smarten up the covers, it would also make a great gift.

1 Cut a strip of cardboard 5cm wider than your photos and long enough to take as many as you want, allowing a 2.5cm border around each one. Fold the card like a concertina to make a separate page for each picture.

2 To make decorative front and back covers, cut two pieces of card about 5mm larger all round than the ends of the concertina. Cover the front and back covers in patterned paper or fabric. Cut the paper or fabric 1cm larger all round than the card and glue in place, fold the edges over to the wrong side and mitre them neatly at the corners before sticking in place.

3 Glue the covers to the end pages of the concertina, trapping lengths of narrow ribbon in-between to act as a tie. Fix your pictures in place with photo corners.

Down memory lane

If your hoard of memorabilia is out of control, it's time to invest in some business-like boxes and files. Brown cardboard is cheap, functional and just waiting for that personal touch, so pull out a few of your mementos and use them to customize plain containers. Favourite postcards, stamps and even old letters can all be stuck on collage-fashion.

1 Collect pictures, stamps or any other suitable materials and decide how you want to arrange them on the box. Lay them in place and make light pencil marks on the box at the corners of each item to use as a guide when sticking.

2 Remove the items and apply PVA adhesive to the back of each one using the artist's brush. Stick them onto the box using the pencil marks as a guide. Wipe away any excess glue immediately (although as PVA adhesive dries clear, small amounts shouldn't show). Leave to dry for approximately 10 minutes.

3 Label the boxes with the names of their contents using Letraset, tracing over the letters with the pencil to transfer them to the box. Carefully erase any obvious pencil marks. Finally, pour a little clear, quick-drying acrylic varnish into a dish and paint over your design. For greater protection, apply one or more coats to the entire surface of the box. Leave to dry.

TIP
Try sticking on items that relate to the contents of each container, such as pressed leaves for a box of gardening paraphernalia or a family photo to decorate one full of sentimental snaps.

In the bag

Too many boxes and cupboards? Soften up on storage by hiding clutter away in a generously sized laundry bag. Choose a fabric that matches the colours of your room scheme and it will look great hanging from a hook in your bedroom or bathroom. If you want to use the same instructions to make a washbag or gift bag, simply use smaller pieces of fabric.

1 Cut front and back panels measuring 65 × 49cm, one casing of 7.5 × 125cm and two ties measuring 5 × 165cm. Place the front and back panels right sides together and stitch 1.5cm from the sides and bottom edge, leaving a 4cm gap on each side, 11.5cm from the top. Trim seams at corners and turn to right side.

TIP
If you want to save time, use cord or ribbons for the drawstring instead of making one from fabric.

2 Turn under a double 1cm hem around the top edge of the bag and stitch. Sew the short ends of the casing together to form a circle, then press under 1.5cm along both raw edges. Place the casing inside the bag, with wrong sides facing, so that it covers the 4cm slots. Pin and stitch to the bag close to the pressed edges of the casing.

3 Press under 1cm along both long edges of each tie, then fold in half lengthways with wrong sides facing and stitch the pressed edges together. Turn in the short raw ends of the ties and hand sew to neaten. Thread ties into slots at sides of bag and through casings. Knot tie ends together to make the drawstring.

Shelf improvement

Take a cheap shelf unit and transform it into an eye-catching storage system for kitchenware. A coat of paint turns rough-looking wood to slick white, and hooks for mugs and rails for utensils help to maximize storage potential.

1 Prepare a wooden unit for painting by filling any holes, then applying primer. Leave to dry, then sand smooth. Apply one or two coats of white gloss paint, leaving each to dry.

2 Use a handsaw to cut dowelling to fit under the top shelf, across the width of the unit. In a well-ventilated space, spray silver paint onto the dowelling and a wire basket, and leave to dry. Screw two large cup hooks under the top shelf, 1cm in from the edge on each side. Fix dowelling between the hooks as a utensil rail. Slot the basket over the third shelf.

3 Mark positions for more cup hooks on the underside of one shelf. Use a bradawl to make a small hole at each mark, then screw them in.

4 Measure the space between the bottom two shelves. Add 2cm to the height and 15cm to the width and cut PVC fabric to this size. Fold in 2cm along one long edge, stick down and attach the eyelets, spaced 10cm apart. Thread the PVC onto net curtain wire, then fix under the bottom shelf using the hooks supplied with the wire.

TIP
Eyelets can be bought in a kit, which comes complete with the necessary hole punch and instructions on how to insert them.

Retro cut

Give a simple shelf unit a groovy retro look with a pair of oval cut-outs. The shelf and brackets are easy to make from MDF and the ovals can be cut out using a jigsaw. A coat of coloured paint completes the look, to create a unit that makes an eye-catching display feature in its own right.

1 Draw an oval shape on card and cut around it to make a template. Cut two squares of 2cm-thick MDF. Place the template on each MDF square so that its length runs from corner to corner, and draw around it. Wearing a mask, cut out the shape using a jigsaw.

2 Cut a panel of MDF for the top of the shelf. Paint the shelf and brackets in the colour and finish of your choice. Emulsion will dry to a flat finish, satinwood will give a mid-sheen effect and gloss paint will produce a shiny look. Leave to dry.

3 Fix the brackets to the wall, then place the shelf across the top and glue in place.

File fiesta

Make your home office a more cheerful place to work and every day will seem like a holiday. Start with a line-up of colourful magazine files; sturdy wooden ones are ideal for tidying up papers and books. Slapping on a coat of paint would be the quickest way of jazzing them up, but these are coloured using a mixture of dye and methylated spirit. This produces a less opaque finish than emulsion or gloss would give, and allows the grain of the wood to show through.

1 Rub down the wood with fine-grade sandpaper to remove any glue residues or varnish. Wearing rubber gloves, pierce a tin of cold water dye, pour the contents into a glass measuring jug and add 250ml of warm water. Dissolve the dye in the water, then add 250ml of methylated spirit and stir well.

2 Paint the colour onto the magazine files using a small paintbrush or sponge. Add further coats if you want a greater intensity of colour. Place the files on paper towels and allow them to dry thoroughly. Finish by applying a coat of protective varnish.

Box room

Old shoe boxes make handy containers for all kinds of bits and pieces. Covering them with fabric means you can keep them on display rather than stashing them away in a cupboard. The fabric that smartens up this box has been tie-dyed, and the lid is padded with wadding to give a soft finish.

1 Wash and iron a length of white, unfinished cotton, then weigh it to find out how much cold water dye you need. To form the pattern shown here, pleat the fabric in concertina style and bind it firmly with thread at 4cm intervals. To dye the fabric, follow the instructions for steps 3 and 4 of the tie-dyed tablecloth project on page 82.

2 When the dyed fabric is dry, cut a panel long enough to go around all four sides of the box, allowing about 5cm extra in the width for turnings at the top and bottom edges. Cover the box with spray adhesive and stick the fabric in place, gluing the top turnings to the inside of the box and the bottom turnings to the base.

3 Cut a piece of wadding the same size as the lid and glue it in place on top. Cut fabric to cover the lid and wadding, again allowing for turnings. Stick the fabric in place on one long side of the lid, then pull it taut over the wadding and glue the opposite side. Repeat for the two shorter sides, folding the fabric in neatly at the corners.

Magnetic attraction

Add a metal strip along the front edge of a shelf, and you can use the phenomenon of magnetism to make it double up as a noticeboard. Gather a selection of fridge magnets to hold reminders and postcards in place on the metal surface. As well as being a practical idea, this also provides a stylish finishing touch for a standard shelf – here shiny stainless steel gives this simple contemporary design a particularly sleek look.

1 Buy a strip of stainless steel that matches the thickness of the shelf, and cut away any excess length. If you buy it from a metal merchant or builders' merchant, ask them if they can cut it to size for you.

2 Squeeze strong adhesive all along the edge of the shelf, or use sturdy double-sided tape. Press the stainless steel strip firmly in place and wipe away any excess glue. If necessary, use tape to keep the strip in position while the glue is drying.

Get stuck in

Découpage is the art of decorating surfaces with paper cutouts, and all it requires is an eye for combining shapes and colours, plus a little careful cutting and pasting. Anyone can create a masterpiece such as this box, which is covered in handmade paper and flower motifs cut from giftwrap. Just make sure you have the right scissors for the job: small, sharp ones such as manicure scissors are essential for tackling the intricate outlines of the flower motifs, while deckle-edged scissors give the mauve stripes their rough-looking edges. A flat paste brush is also useful, to help you get an even spread of glue.

TIP
Plain wooden accessories and furniture designed for home painting or decorating (known as blanks) are available from specialist mail order suppliers – see Stockists on page 210 for details.

1 Using paper glue, cover a wooden box and lid with natural-coloured handmade paper, overlapping it at the edges. Trim the edges with a craft knife. Cover the lid edges with strips of mauve handmade paper. Cut narrow strips of mauve paper using deckle-edged scissors and arrange them on the box and lid in a lattice design. Fix securely in place using paper glue.

2 Using sharp manicure scissors, carefully cut flower motifs from giftwrap and stick them to the box, one by one. Brush glue onto the box, press a flower in place and smooth from the centre to the edges to remove air bubbles. Wipe off any excess glue with a damp sponge.

3 When the glue is dry, seal the whole box with two coats of clear acrylic varnish, sanding lightly after each coat.

Under cover

Don't throw out those old telephone directories when the new ones arrive on your doorstep. Recycle their pages by using them to cover plain boxes, then stack a set together for smart storage. The paper is torn into strips and applied with wallpaper paste using papier-mâché techniques, which means you can use the standard directory pages to cover boxes of any size. If you would prefer your covering to be a little more colourful, try using giftwrap or pages torn from old books or magazines.

Look for sturdy cardboard or wooden boxes.

1 Cover your work surface with newspaper, then prepare some wallpaper paste following the manufacturer's instructions.

2 Tear up strips of paper and coat each one with paste by dipping it in, then running it through your fingers to remove any excess. Smooth the strips one by one onto the boxes and lids, overlapping the edges, until they are covered with paper. Leave to dry.

TIP
If you make up too much wallpaper paste, any excess can be stored in a jar with a screw-top lid until you next want to use it.

Glad hatters

Even if you don't have hats to keep in them, hatboxes make great storage solutions. Capacious enough to gobble up out-of-season clothes or excess bedlinen, their attractive shapes mean you can leave them perched on top of a wardrobe or in the corner of a bedroom without feeling that they spoil the view. Decorative hatboxes can be wildly expensive to buy, but plain cardboard ones are cheaper and easy to decorate. A pretty rose stamp and pink ribbon handles give these plain white boxes a lift, and a larger version of the same stamp is repeated on the wall behind.

1 Buy a small rubber stamp from a DIY store or craft shop. Some stamp manufacturers sell special stamp paint, but you could also use stencil paints.

Pour a small amount of paint into a dish or old saucer and use a brush or stamp roller to apply a thin, even coat to the raised surface of the stamp. Carefully press the stamp onto the hatbox, then lift off. Repeat until the box is covered with motifs, spacing them evenly.

2 If you are using two colours with one stamp, it is best to stamp each colour separately. For example, stamp all the roses in pink and leave to dry, then stamp the leaves in green, making sure you line up the stamp properly with the first part of the motif.

3 Complete your hatbox makeover by cutting a length of narrow ribbon, threading it through the holes to make a handle, and knotting the ends on the inside.

Neat seat

Add an upholstered lid, padded with foam, and a wooden storage box doubles up as a comfy bench. You can buy foam rubber from specialist suppliers (see your local phone book) who will usually cut it to size.

1 Lightly sand the box, apply primer, then paint using gloss or eggshell. Remove lid. Make a paper template of the lid and get foam rubber cut to this size.

2 Lay newspaper on the floor, and cover one side of the foam with a spray adhesive designed for foam. Position foam glue side down on lid and leave to dry. Measure the lid, taking the tape down to the timber. Cut medium-weight wadding and calico to these dimensions. Cut top fabric 2cm larger all round.

3 Place the wadding over the foam and cover with the calico, folding in and tacking corners neatly. Centre the fabric over the calico and use a staple

gun, or tacks and a hammer, to attach it to the side edges of the lid. Work on opposite sides, keeping the fabric straight and spacing the tacks 10 to 15cm apart. Check the result, and re-hammer any tacks if necessary.

4 Trim excess fabric level with edge of lid. Position braid to cover raw edges of fabric and align with lowest edges of lid. Hammer tacks in around sides of box lid, catching in braid and main fabric. Where the braid joins, fold in raw edges and butt join it, hiding join with a tack. Refit lid.

TIP
Upholstery materials should be fire-resistant. Check that the foam and fabric you choose comply with current safety regulations.

Drill thrill

Here's your chance to go crazy with a drill! With a variety of bits, you can add pierced and dot designs to furniture and storage boxes. This style of decoration particularly suits painted wood because the even surface shows off the pattern well, so it is a useful way of revamping old furniture or personalizing MDF blanks. In this bathroom, the laundry bin, medicine cabinet and waste bin have all been given the drill treatment, showing just a few of the designs you can achieve.

1 Before tackling furnishings, practise on scrap timber. Work on a stable surface, such as a workbench, clamp the wood down and place another piece of wood under the one you are working on. Hold the drill steady, with the bit at a 90° angle to the wood. Experiment with different drill bits: a hole saw attachment will cut doorknob-sized holes, flat wood bits are for medium holes, and wood drill bits come in dozens of sizes. A single countersink bit will bore cone-shaped indentations in a variety of sizes; the harder you press down, the wider and deeper the hollow.

2 When you have a design in mind, lightly sand the wood of the item to be drilled. Mark out the design on the wood using light pencil marks, then do the drilling. Sand or file around your drilled holes.

3 Apply a coat of primer and leave to dry, then add a top coat of emulsion or satinwood in the colour of your choice. If using emulsion, finish with a coat of clear varnish.

TIP
Keep your practice boards and label the holes with the drill bit sizes in case you want to repeat the same design in future.

Waxing lyrical

Batik is a craft that works on the principle of 'resist dyeing'. Warm wax is used to draw a design on fabric, which is then dyed. Waxed areas resist the dye, so that when the wax is removed the pattern remains. The pattern for this cushion cover is taken from a body art transfer kit, but you can use any design you like.

1 Following the manufacturer's instructions, and wearing rubber gloves, mix orange cold water dye with fixative and salt. Add water to cover a length of white cotton. Wash the fabric, and submerge in the dye while still wet. Leave for an hour, agitating regularly, then remove and rinse until the water runs clear. Leave to dry, then iron.

2 Enlarge your design on a photocopier if necessary, then centre the fabric flat over the design. Heat batik wax in a small saucepan, placed over a larger one of simmering water. Using

a tool called a tjanting or a very fine paintbrush, trace over the design through the fabric with the wax. When the wax has hardened, dye the fabric red, as in step 1. Leave to dry.

3 Place the fabric between sheets of kitchen paper and press with a very hot iron. The wax will melt onto the paper. Repeat until no more wax is absorbed. Wash and iron the fabric. Cut it to fit your cushion pad, adding a 1.5cm seam allowance. Stitch three sides, insert pad and slipstitch closed. Make a second cover from organza, 5cm larger all round.

TIP
After drawing on your design, check the underside of the fabric to ensure that the wax has been absorbed right through and is not just sitting on the surface.

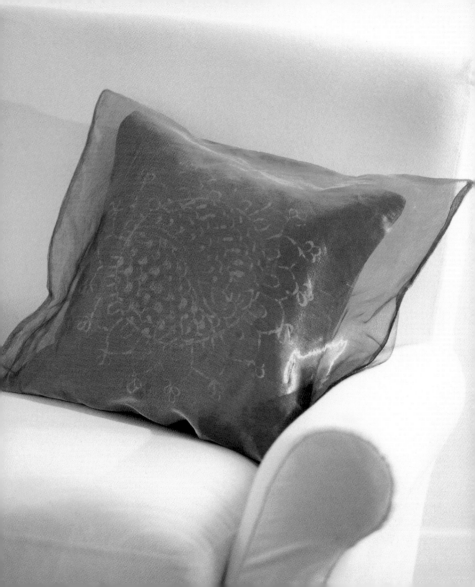

Table topper

If an ugly or shabby table is letting your decor down and you can't afford to replace it, do a hide-and-disguise job by running up a simple fabric cover. Loose furniture covers not only conceal a multitude of sins but can also be a quick and easy way of adding a splash of colour to a neutral scheme. For a room with solid furniture, choose heavy wool, brocade or damask, but go for pretty chintz and lighter fabrics for a bright, airy look.

1 Measure your tabletop and add 3cm to the length and width. Cut the top of your cover to these measurements. Cut four skirt pieces – the ones shown here are 28cm deep, including 3.5cm for seams. Two pieces should be the same length as the cover and two the same as the width. Sew the skirt pieces together along their short sides, leaving 1.5cm open at the tops of the seams. Press seams open.

2 Stitch a 1cm double hem around the lower edge of the skirt. Pin and stitch the skirt to the cover with right sides facing and raw edges matching. Make sure that each seam of the skirt lines up with a corner of the cover.

3 Stitch the skirt to the cover, allowing the top of the skirt seams to open as you go around each corner. Trim off the corners diagonally to reduce bulk, taking care not to cut the stitching. Press seams down towards the skirt. Turn right side out and place over your table.

TIP
Make sure the fabric you choose for a table cover is washable. Alternatively, lay a piece of glass over the top, cut to fit by a glazier.

Cushy numbers

Mounds of cushions piled on a sofa, armchair or bed give a room an inviting feel. If you know how to make a basic cushion cover, it's easy to adapt the design to create any number of individual looks. For example, you could choose fabrics in different colours for the front and back, to provide a stunning contrast. Or you could have the opening at the front and fasten it with decorative buttons, eyelets, toggles or ties. Follow the instructions below to make a simple envelope-style cover for a square or rectangular pad.

1 Cut one front panel the size of the cushion pad, adding 3cm to the length and width for seam allowances. Cut one back panel the same size, plus 15cm for the overlap of the envelope.

2 Fold the back panel in half widthways, and then cut it along the fold into two identical pieces. Stitch a 1cm double hem on both these cut edges.

3 Place the back panels and front panel together, with right sides facing and raw edges matching, so that the back panels overlap by 11cm at the centre. Stitch a 1.5cm seam around the outer edges. Trim the seams at the corners to reduce bulk, then turn the cover right side out and press. Slip over the cushion pad.

Bedtime bliss

Ensure that all your dreams are sweet ones by trimming pillowcases and duvet covers with candy-coloured ribbons and bows. Or if that's a bit too girly for your taste, choose from the wide array of ribbons and braids on sale in haberdashery stores to reflect your own style. How about masculine tartans or sumptuous jewel-coloured velvets instead? Plain white bedlinen is just crying out for that personal touch.

1 To decorate pillowcases, choose a selection of wide and narrow ribbon or braid and ready-made bows. Cut the ribbon slightly longer than the width of the pillowcase and pin in place, turning under the ends to neaten. Machine sew close to the ribbon edges using matching sewing thread. Alternatively, sew small ready-made bows to the pillowcase, spacing them evenly. If you wish, sew ribbons to the open edges of the case and tie in bows.

2 To decorate a duvet cover to match, choose narrow ribbon in four different colours. Cut the ribbon into 40cm lengths, knot each piece in the centre and tie into a neat bow. Pin the bows to the duvet cover and sew the knots in place, taking care not to sew through both layers of the cover.

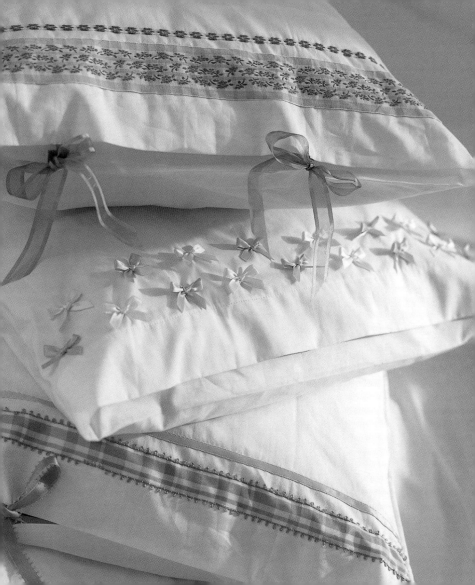

Soft option

Snuggle up with cushion covers made from soft, stretchy fleece fabric. Vibrant colours add warmth to a light-coloured sofa and, as fleece fabric doesn't fray, it's easy to combine a mix of contrasting hues to create bold appliqué designs.

1 Measure your cushion pad and cut green fabric for the cover front – don't allow extra for seams as the cover will stretch to fit. Cut a panel of grey fabric about 16cm wide to fit across the front, and an orange strip 3 × 22cm.

2 Pin the orange strip along the centre of the grey panel. Using orange thread and a medium zigzag setting on your machine, stitch the strip in place by sewing close to, but not over, its edges. Pin then stitch the grey panel onto the centre of the cover front, using the same zigzag setting and matching thread.

3 For the back, cut two panels of green fabric, each the same width as the front cover in one direction and two-thirds of the width in the other. Stitch a 2cm hem along one longer edge of each. Lay out the cover front, appliqué side up, then place the back pieces on top, right side down, aligning raw edges with those of the front and overlapping hemmed edges at the centre. Pin then stitch the front and backs together with a 1cm seam allowance. Trim one layer of the allowance and clip corners, then turn right side out. Press seams flat, using a cool setting on your iron, and insert the cushion pad.

TIP
The stretchiness of fleece fabric can make it difficult to cut to size, so you may find it easier to make paper patterns for the cover and appliqué pieces.

Patch it up

A patchwork throw will bring a touch of traditional charm to any bedroom. You don't need to spend hours hand-stitching tiny pieces of fabric; with large squares the sewing machine can do all the work. These instructions make a throw of about 110 × 150cm.

1 Cut 22cm squares from strong paper to make patterns, and use to cut seven squares from each of five coordinating fabrics. Arrange the squares right side up in rows of five across and seven down, alternating the fabrics.

2 Stitch each horizontal row of squares together into a strip, with right sides facing and 1cm seam allowances. Press seam allowances open. Lay the strips right side up in their correct positions. Pin them together, pinning through the corresponding vertical seam lines to make sure they match. Stitch the strips together.

3 For the border, cut two 7 × 142cm strips and two 7 × 112cm strips from a sixth fabric. With right sides facing, stitch a long strip to each long edge of the rectangle, with 1cm seam allowances. Next, stitch a shorter strip to each short edge and across the tops of the borders already stitched.

4 Cut a 112 × 152cm piece of backing fabric. With right sides facing, lay the patchwork on it and pin together around all edges. Trim any excess backing, then stitch, leaving a gap in one edge. Snip across seam allowances at the corners and turn right side out. Press edges flat and slipstitch gap.

TIP
For the best results with patchwork, use closely woven fabrics that are all of equal weights – printed cottons are ideal for this throw.

Feet first

Sink your toes into a luxurious towelling bath mat. Quilted to give it a soft, springy feel, this mat is lined with fusible volume fleece, available from haberdashers. This adheres to one piece of towelling, making it easy to keep the layers together when sewing the quilted lines. Striped cotton finishes the edges and provides a smart border.

1 Cut two pieces of towelling and one piece of fusible volume fleece, each measuring 53 × 75cm. Following the manufacturer's instructions, fuse the fleece to one piece of towelling. With the fleece sandwiched between them, place the two pieces of towelling together and tack 5cm from the edges to mark the border area.

2 With the fused side up, use tailor's chalk to draw a diagonal line between opposite corners. Tack or pin near this line, then machine stitch along it, starting and ending just inside the border. Pin and stitch parallel diagonal lines 12cm apart, then repeat in the other direction, to make a diamond pattern.

3 From contrasting cotton fabric, cut two 17.5 × 75cm and two 17.5 × 67cm strips. With right sides facing, stitch the long strips to the long edges of the mat, 5cm from the edge. Press under 1.5cm on the loose edges, fold to reverse of mat and slipstitch to the machine stitches. With the short strips extending 1.5cm beyond each end, bind the short edges in the same way. Tuck under and slipstitch ends.

Splash catcher

Hand towels sewn together patchwork-style make a distinctive shower curtain. Pick up a bundle of towels at bargain prices in the sales, choosing two contrasting colours for a simple but striking effect. Back them with proper shower-curtain fabric to ensure that the finished result is waterproof.

1 Lay out the towels in a chequerboard pattern, overlapping the edges slightly. Towels have a nap, or pile, which can affect the depth of colour, so make sure this runs in the same direction on all the towels of one colour – to check, run your hand up and down them and one direction will feel rough, the other smooth. Pin and topstitch each horizontal row together, then stitch the rows to one another, aligning the vertical seams.

2 Fold the top edge of the curtain 5cm to the wrong side and insert eyelets following the manufacturer's instructions. Space them evenly, adjusting the spacing if necessary to avoid the seams.

3 To make the waterproof backing, hem the shower-curtain fabric so that it is the same size, giving it a top hem of 3-5cm. With wrong sides facing, lay it on the towelling curtain and mark positions for eyelets on the lining, matching them to those on the towelling. Insert eyelets in the lining and hang the curtain with hooks or rings through both sets of eyelets.

TIP
Towels are thick to sew, so use a heavy-duty needle in your sewing machine, such as a jeans needle.

Bath attendant

A towelling and gingham slipcover turns a plain chair into practical and attractive bathroom seating. Buttoned tabs mean this cover can easily be removed for washing.

1 Make a pattern by placing paper on the chair seat and creasing it along the edges. Use a ruler to draw the crease lines, then use a set square to draw a 12cm skirt from each line. The corners are cut away, so the final pattern should look like a squat cross. Add 1cm seam allowances to the cut-away corners, cut out the pattern and use it to cut one cover from towelling and one from lining.

2 Cut eight 7 × 18cm tabs with pointed ends from gingham, and four from interfacing. Fuse interfacing tabs to wrong side of four gingham tabs. For binding, cut 6cm-wide bias strips of gingham. Press long edges 1.2cm to wrong side.

3 With right sides facing, stitch tabs together in pairs, leaving unpointed ends open. Trim corners, turn right side out and press flat. Work a 22mm buttonhole on each, starting 2.5cm from the point. Pin tabs to front and back skirts, matching raw edges. With right sides facing and a 1cm seam allowance, stitch towelling to lining at each cut-away corner, catching in tabs. Snip diagonally into seam allowances at corners. Turn to right side and press.

4 Tack cover to lining at loose skirt edges. Open out binding strips. With right sides facing, raw edges matching and binding extending 1cm beyond skirt ends, pin binding strips to skirt edges and stitch along foldline. Fold pressed edges of binding to lining side and slipstitch to machine stitches, tucking in ends at corners. Sew on buttons to hold tabs in place.

Easy elegance

Very little sewing is needed to create these luxurious-looking bolster covers, as the fabric is simply knotted at the ends for a decorative effect. Silks in bright colours create a sumptuous feel. Dupion silk is just the right weight as it is fine enough to knot easily yet has enough body to make the ends frill out attractively.

1 To assess how long the cover needs to be, pin silk around your bolster pad, allowing plenty of excess fabric at one end. Mark the point where the bolster ends using tailor's chalk, then knot the excess fabric. Allow enough beyond the knot to form a flamboyant frill and make another mark at the end of the frill. It's best to allow a bit too much at this stage, as a frill that is too small will spoil the effect; you can always trim it later. Measure between the two marks to find the length of each end section. Multiply this by two, then add the length of the bolster pad plus 4cm for hems to find the overall length of the cover. To find the width, measure around your bolster pad and add 3cm for seams. Cut silk to these dimensions.

2 Fold the fabric in half lengthways and sew the two long edges together with a 1.5cm seam allowance to create a fabric tube. Turn up and stitch 1cm double hems at each end. Place the bolster pad inside, position it and knot the fabric at either end.

TIP
Use the whole width of the fabric and you won't have to hem the ends, as the silk should already be finished at its side edges.

Fern favourite

Customize a linen table runner with an elegant fern motif, applied using silver foil. The silver blends beautifully with this icy blue, adding a sophisticated glimmer to a simple glass-topped table. This effect could also be used to give plain duvet sets or ready-made curtains a dazzling revamp. The fern motif is created by using a prepared stencil, but if you feel artistic you could design your own or even apply the glue and foil freehand.

1 Lay one end of the runner out on a flat surface and position the stencil on top. Hold it in place with masking tape, then dab all over the cut-out areas with appliqué glue. Leave to dry for one hour only.

2 Place a sheet of appliqué foil over the motif and rub it in firmly so that it adheres to the glue. Remove and reposition the foil sheet until the whole of the motif has been covered. Repeat the process to make a second metallic motif on the other end of the runner. When ironing, press on the wrong side.

Smart set

Have the most stylish table settings in town with place mats that are sure to impress your guests. Complete with their own cutlery pockets, these have the luxurious look of real suede. They are simple to sew, and although the 'suede' looks expensive, it is in fact a realistic lookalike that is a more affordable option and widely available from fabric shops.

1 For each mat, cut out a piece of faux suede measuring about 26 × 32cm. Press and stitch a double 1cm hem around the edges to create a neat, soft line. Mitre the corners to make the hem sit flat. To do this, fold under the whole corner on the diagonal before hemming, and trim off most of the triangle, leaving just 1cm from the diagonal fold line. Then, when you turn under the 1cm double hems on the straight sides, their ends should meet neatly at the corner.

2 To make the cutlery pocket, cut another piece of fabric measuring 13 × 17cm. Press under 1cm around all edges and stitch across the top edge to hem. Position the pocket on the mat and stitch around the remaining three sides.

TIP
White linen napkins and plain white tableware will reinforce this look of stylish simplicity. Make matching rings for napkins by tying them with a length of brown ribbon.

Colour boost

Cheer up mealtimes with a dash of colour by using dyes to give your table linen a lift. Once a boring beige, this raffia place mat is now an eye-popping pink, and there are many more colour ranges to choose from. Cold water hand dyes are available from haberdashery stores, and work best on natural fibres.

1 Weigh the mat to work out how much dye is required. You will need one 100g packet of hand dye for every 250g of dry weight. First wash the mat – dye it while still damp.

2 To mix the dye, put on rubber gloves and empty the packet of dye into a large glass container, such as a measuring jug. Add 1ltr of hot water and stir well. Fill a second, shallow container, large enough to take the unfolded mat, with 6ltr hot water (the temperature should be about 60°C) and 250g salt. Add the dye solution and stir well.

3 Submerge the damp mat in the dye bath, then agitate and squeeze it at regular intervals to ensure that the colour penetrates all the way through. After an hour, rinse the mat under a cold tap until the water runs clear. Wash separately with detergent.

TIP
If you want to change the colour of larger items, such as a tablecloth, you may find it easier to choose a machine dye, which can be used in your washing machine.

Simply groovy

A familiar sight on hippie T-shirts, tie-dying can also create brilliant patterns on home furnishings. Take a plain white tablecloth in a fine, even-weave natural fabric, and have fun pleating, tying and knotting to make a combination of designs. Choose any dye colour you like, although patterns show up best against stronger shades, such as this indigo.

1 Most fabrics have a finish that must be removed before they can be dyed. To do this, wash in warm water with soap flakes (some fabrics, such as cotton, may have to be boiled before they will lose their finish). Leave the cloth to dry, then iron. Weigh it to find out how much dye you need – see dye packet for quantities.

2 Pleat, tie or knot the fabric to create the patterns you want. For small circles, tie stones or marbles into the fabric, or for larger circles, draw the fabric

into a peak and bind with thread. Make the border around the edge by pleating the fabric and placing paper clips side by side over the fold. The pattern on top is formed by pinning folds of fabric with safety pins.

3 When all the tying is done, wet the fabric thoroughly. Prepare the dye following the manufacturer's instructions and, wearing rubber gloves, submerge the cloth in the dye. Leave for up to an hour, stirring regularly.

4 Remove the cloth and rinse in cold water until the water runs clear. Wash in warm water and detergent. Remove the ties and hang the tablecloth out to dry.

TIP
Although dyed items will be colourfast, it is safer to wash them separately for the first few times after dyeing to remove any residue.

Breakfast news

Ditch the tablecloth, and instead give yourself something to read while munching your toast and cereal. Decorate your tabletop with newspaper cuttings, postcards or pages cut from an old book – how about a cookery book for some culinary inspiration? If you and your family always sit in the same places, you could include a name at each place setting. If you have chairs with smooth wooden backs, try decorating these to match.

1 Gather the materials you want to paper the table with, then decide how you want to arrange them. Using a paint-brush, apply PVA adhesive to the back of each piece. Stick them in place on the tabletop, over-lapping the edges to give perfect coverage. Continue them down over the side edges of the table, wiping away excess glue immediately.

2 When the table is completely covered, leave until the glue is dry. To protect the paperwork, apply one or more coats of clear acrylic varnish to the entire surface, ensuring it is dry between coats.

Checkmate

An unassuming wooden chair gets a personality boost with some lively mosaic-style paintwork. Choose a selection of toning shades that suit your room scheme to paint a chequerboard design on a flat or curved chair back. You could use the same idea to jazz up a cupboard front or tabletop.

1 Sand the back of the chair, and apply undercoat. When this is dry, paint it with two coats of your lightest colour, using satin finish paint. Measure the chair back and work out how many 2.5cm squares will fit across and down (if it does not divide exactly, adjust the size of the squares to fit). Mark out the squares using a ruler and pencil, continuing them over the edges of the back. If your chair has a curved back, use a flexible ruler.

2 Using a square-ended artist's brush, apply the remaining colours in a random pattern. Working from the lightest to the darkest, apply one colour at a time, painting all the squares in that shade and leaving them to dry before starting on the next. Wash the brush well between colours. When the last set of squares is dry, apply two coats of clear matt acrylic varnish to finish.

TIP
As you only need small amounts of each shade, buy sample pots of satin finish paint or, for all except the basecoat, tubes of concentrated artists' acrylics.

Shore thing

Conjure up memories of fresh sea air and walks along the coast by re-creating a little piece of shingle beach in your own home. Take a collection of smooth, flat pebbles and use them to make an unusual decorative tabletop. The pebbles are arranged in a metal tray mounted on a stand, where they are set in plaster of Paris.

1 If your tray is too deep, place a sheet of MDF in the base. Choose flat pebbles, wash and dry them thoroughly if

collected from the beach, and arrange them in the tray. Glue the stones one by one onto the MDF or tray base using strong epoxy adhesive. Leave the glue to harden thoroughly.

2 Cover your work surface with newspaper and mix plaster of Paris in a jug to the consistency of single cream. Pour this between the pebbles until it comes halfway up them, filling in all the spaces. Wipe off spills with a damp cloth at once. Leave overnight to harden, then clean off any drips with steel wool.

3 Finish by applying two coats of polyurethane varnish with a soft paintbrush – use matt varnish for the white stones and satin on the dark ones, to bring out the colours.

Quick silver

Make inexpensive wooden chairs shine with a few coats of silver spray paint, and they'll look classy enough for any dining room. With the money you save on the chairs, splash out on a glass-topped table and some stylish new chrome accessories to create a cool, contemporary look.

1 Make sure that the surface of your chair is clean and dry. Sand smooth furniture that has been previously painted or varnished, or give new wood two coats of primer.

2 To apply the spray paint, work outdoors or in a well-ventilated room where you have plenty of space.

Cover the surrounding area with a dustsheet or lots of newspaper. For the best results, apply three light coats of silver or chrome spray paint; don't be tempted to cut corners by using one heavy coat. Leave until thoroughly dry, then buff the painted surface with a soft cloth to bring up the shine.

TIP
Hints of soft pink will warm up a silver scheme. Add bought seat pads covered in pink fabric or make your own, using foam as the base.

Stripe it bright

Adding an element of pattern can lift even the most boring room scheme out of the doldrums, and jazzing up a plain tabletop can do a lot to cheer up a dreary kitchen, without the need for major redecoration of walls or units. Stripes in toning shades give a bright, modern look, and are easy to paint onto a plain wooden table. Yellow is an ideal colour choice for instant cheer, guaranteed to raise the spirits.

1 If possible, choose a table with a surface that is untreated, ie unwaxed and unvarnished.

Otherwise, sand down the surface before you start to provide a key for the paint, then apply a basecoat of emulsion in a light neutral colour and leave to dry.

2 Apply masking tape of varying widths down the length of the table, making sure that the lines are straight. Using sample pots of yellow and white emulsion, paint stripes between the tapes. Leave until thoroughly dry, then carefully remove the tape. To finish, apply two coats of clear acrylic varnish.

TIP
To skip the chore of sanding down old furniture, apply a multi-surface primer. These are designed to cover any previous finish and provide a paintable surface.

Leather look

Dress up a cheap wooden table in a leather jacket and it will be able to strut its stuff in the most stylish of room settings. As well as giving the furniture a more expensive look, leather has a luxuriously tactile surface. Dark leather would suit a period-style room, but white blends in well with light contemporary interiors. The base and legs of this plain wooden table have been painted white to match. Upholstery tacks with a bronze finish add a decorative finishing touch around the edge.

1 Cut a piece of leather that is large enough to cover your table and also wrap over its edges. Lay it on top of the table, positioning it centrally, then fold one side over the edge and fix to the underside using a staple gun or drawing pins. Pull the opposite edge taut and fix in the same way. Repeat with the remaining two sides, trimming excess leather at the corners and folding them neatly in place.

2 Decorate the edge of the table by hammering in a row of evenly-spaced upholstery tacks.

Appear in print

Painting designs on plywood is easy if you use mono-printing. This simple technique involves painting shapes onto acetate and then printing them onto a surface. Etching designs in the wet paint, or scrubbing it to add texture, allows you to create interesting effects. These lozenge shapes were printed using three shades of blue for a cool, fresh look.

1 Seal an unfinished plywood table with two coats of acrylic gloss varnish. In separate bowls, prepare three paint shades by mixing white emulsion with small amounts of artists' acrylics. Using one shade, paint a lozenge shape on a sheet of acetate. To add texture, scrub the paint hard with a household paintbrush while still wet.

2 Position the acetate, paint side down, on the table. Smooth over the back to transfer the paint to the wood. Work quickly before the emulsion dries. Then carefully peel back the acetate to reveal the print.

3 Print more lozenge shapes using the other shades. To decorate some with spirals or wavy lines, paint the acetate, then mark the design in the wet paint using the end of a rubber-handled brush. Apply to the table as before. Add further interest by including similar shapes in different sizes and by partially overlapping some of the blocks of colour.

4 When the paint is dry, varnish the tabletop and legs with two coats of acrylic varnish.

Clever cube

Whether you use it as a footstool, coffee table or extra seating, this handsome cube will be a versatile addition to your living room. Cover a block of foam rubber with fake suede fabric and you've got a cube that looks just like the trendy leather or suede versions available in the shops – but at a fraction of the price.

1 Ask a foam supplier to cut a cube to size for you – this one measures 50cm. From faux suede fabric, cut a square the same size as one side of the cube, adding 8cm for seam allowances. Using this as a template, cut four more.

2 With right sides facing, sew the five squares together to make a cross shape. Press the seam allowances. Sew the four side seams to form an open cube. Trim seam allowances and turn the cube right side out. If the fabric is the type that frays badly, hem the four raw edges. Squeeze the foam inside.

3 To make a firm base, place a square of board on top of the foam. Pull the raw or hemmed fabric edges taut over the board and fix them in place using a staple gun. Use the cube with the board at the bottom.

Cabinet reshuffle

This pretty cupboard looks like a hand-painted piece that has stood the test of time, but in fact its aged look is the result of a distressed paint effect, and the floral design on the door has been applied using transfer glaze. This clever substance allows you to choose any picture you like and reproduce it on another surface simply by brushing on the glaze to form a transfer.

1 Sand down your cabinet to remove any previous finish, then paint it all over with a mid-tone shade of green or blue. Leave to dry, then rub candlewax on areas that might suffer wear and tear, such as the panel edges. Apply a coat of white or cream paint on top then, when dry, rub back the waxed areas with wire wool to expose glimpses of the coloured base coat.

2 To create the image, find a picture you like. This should be on paper and the right size to cover the front of the cabinet – enlarge it using a photocopier if necessary. Paint transfer glaze over the face of your picture, brushing it on vertically. When dry, add another coat, applied horizontally. Add two more coats, one in each direction, then leave to dry for two hours.

3 Soak the image in warm water, with the print face down, for 20 minutes. Then remove the print and place it face down on the cupboard door. Peel the paper away using your fingertips, leaving the image and glaze behind. Seal by painting with transfer glaze.

TIP
If you prefer a top coat in a darker colour, simply reverse the order in which the shades are applied, using white or cream as a contrasting base coat.

Second sitting

Re-upholstering a drop-in seat pad can give an old chair a new lease of life. This one is padded with wadding, lined with calico and covered with furnishing fabric. You'll need a hammer and small tacks or a staple gun suitable for light work.

1 Remove the seat pad and use a chisel or pliers to prise out tacks or staples securing the existing fabric. If the pad is damaged, replace it with new foam cut to size. If not, brush it down. Measure the seat pad, taking the tape right around to the wooden frame. Cut a template from tracing paper, adding 5cm all round, and use to cut this shape from wadding, calico and furnishing fabric.

2 Lay the calico out and place the wadding then the seat pad on top. Starting from the centre back, fold the calico up onto the frame and staple or tack in the centre of each side. Making sure the fabric is straight, staple or tack all along one edge, working from the centre outwards. Repeat for the opposite edge, pulling the fabric taut. Fix adjoining sides, then trim wadding and calico back to the tacks or staples.

3 Repeat step 2 using the furnishing fabric. At the corners, fold the fabric into neat mitres, checking it's smooth on top.

4 Cut calico to cover the base of the seat pad and press under 1cm around all edges. Tack or staple in place on the underside of the pad. Replace seat pad.

Twenties revival

Re-create the glamorous mirrored fashion of the 1920s by adding a reflective top to a pretty period-style table. Look for a suitable piece of furniture in a junk shop or blank furniture suppliers. You can create the exact look you want by giving it a complete makeover with a lick of paint and a beautiful new drawer handle as well.

1 If you are revamping a table that is varnished or polished, either sand it down well to provide a key for the paint or apply a coat of multi-surface primer. Paint every surface, except those to be covered with mirrors, with satin finish in the colour of your choice.

2 Measure or make a template of the surfaces to be mirrored – the top of the table and the front of the drawer. Ask a local glazier to cut pieces of mirror to the required size, and also to polish the edges and drill a hole for a drawer handle. Apply specialist mirror glue to the tabletop and drawer front and press the mirrors into position. Leave to dry for at least 24 hours, then attach the drawer handle.

Deck 'em out

If your old deck chair covers are looking faded or tatty, brighten up summer days by making some crisp new ones that simply slip over the top. That means you don't have to spend time removing the old covers or hand-stitching the new ones to the wooden frame. When the slip covers need a wash, all you have to do is peel apart the Velcro fastening and whip them off. Choose firmly woven cotton prints for the best results.

1 Measure the length and width of the existing cover, then cut fabric to the same width plus 4cm, and twice the length plus 8cm. If the fabric you choose is more than twice the width of the cover, you can economize by cutting it in half lengthways and stitching the two pieces together to make up the required length. Press under and stitch a double 1cm hem around all edges.

2 Stitch corresponding strips of Velcro to the wrong side of one short end and the right side of the other end. Loop over the existing cover and secure the Velcro ends together.

Light relief

Bring a new dimension to stencilling by adding wall filler to the paint, giving designs a raised, textured finish. Forget fussy flowers and grapevines, this treatment works best with simple modern motifs such as this abstract leaf design, used to add an eye-catching border around an alcove.

1 Trace a motif onto paper using a soft pencil. Turn the paper over and thickly trace over the outline on the back. Place paper, with this side down, on a sheet of waxed stencil card. Go over the outline to transfer the image onto the card. Place the card on a board or a thick layer of newspaper and carefully cut out the motif using a sharp craft knife.

2 Mix powdered wall filler with a little water so it has a thick and creamy texture, then add acrylic paint in the shade of your choice, a little at a time, until you're happy with the colour. Bear in mind that when it is dry, the mixture will look slightly lighter than when wet.

3 Plan the layout of the motifs on the wall, using a spirit level and ruler to line them up evenly. Tape the stencil lightly to the wall and apply paste over the cutout areas with a short-bristled brush or palette knife. Use a gentle stippling movement so the paste stands up in peaks. Carefully peel back the card to reveal the motif. If paste has bled underneath, allow it to dry, then carefully scratch away with the tip of a craft knife.

TIP
Relief stencilling can also be used to jazz up plain unglazed tiles. In a bathroom or kitchen, protect your work from steam and moisture by applying a coat of acrylic spray varnish.

Floor show

If you want to give wooden floorboards a livelier look, a lick of paint is the answer. The lines of the boards suggest a ready-made pattern, so choose two contrasting shades of satin finish and use them to create dramatic stripes. To avoid too regimented an effect, vary the width of the stripes from one to three boards.

1 To prepare your floorboards, hammer down any protruding nails and rub down sharp edges and splinters. If you have sanded bare boards, apply knotting over the knots, then add a coat of wood primer. When dry, rub down with fine wet-and-dry sandpaper to remove blemishes and wipe over using a cloth dampened with white spirit. Fill any gaps with wood filler. If your boards are varnished, stained or already painted, simply sand the surface, then clean with warm soapy water before painting.

2 Measure your room and count the number of floorboards. Draw a scale version of your design on graph paper – plan the spacing between the stripes by using the boards as a guide.

3 On the floor, mask off all the stripes to be painted in your first colour. Apply two coats of the first paint shade. When this is dry, carefully remove the masking tape. Mask off the remaining boards, apply two coats of the second colour and, when dry, remove the masking tape.

4 Finally, apply two coats of a suitable clear floor varnish to protect the design from wear and tear, leaving it to dry thoroughly between each coat. Do not walk on the floor until it is completely dry.

TIP
Use low-tack masking tape – this will not lift off the paint you have already applied when you mask off the second set of boards.

Rock star

Pebbles and plaster go into the mix to create a fireplace that combines classic drama with more rustic elements. A pair of ornate plaster corbels forms an intriguing contrast with the simple timber mantelshelf, painted and distressed to resemble driftwood. Corbels are available in a wide range of styles, so you can go as plain or elaborate as you want. The unfinished brick interior of the fireplace adds to the rustic appeal, while a semi-circle of concrete set with pebbles makes an attractive seaside-style hearth.

1 Cut a length of timber to size for the mantelshelf and sand down the edges and corners to give a worn look. Paint the timber with white emulsion then, when dry, rub away patches of the paint with wire wool to create a distressed appearance. Fix the shelf to the wall above the fireplace using brackets.

2 Paint the corbels white using fire-resistant paint. When dry, place one corbel over each bracket and glue and screw in place.

3 To make a mould for the pebbly hearth, cut a piece of arched plastic to the width of the hearth, plus at least 15cm on either side. Screw in place at each side of the fire breast. Pour in concrete until level with the plastic and embed a selection of dark and light pebbles in the surface. Leave for 24 hours to set, then remove the mould.

Clear winner

If your bedroom is on the small side, a separate dressing area may seem out of the question, but with this stylish screen you can create an effective partition without losing light. Clear Perspex is decorated with a squared design using etching spray, which creates a finish that looks like frosted glass. The result will provide a degree of privacy for a dressing area, or conceal the chaos of your sewing corner or office space, without making the room seem smaller or darker.

1 Take a sheet of clear Perspex, cut to the size you want – your supplier may be able to do this for you. Cover the Perspex with a grid design of evenly sized squares by sticking on strips of masking tape.

2 Coat the screen all over with etching spray. Work in a well-ventilated area and cover the surrounding surfaces well with a dustsheet or newspaper. Spray on two or three light coats, building up the coverage gradually until you achieve the effect you want. Leave to dry.

3 Remove the masking tape to reveal the design. Drill small holes at the top of the screen and hang it from the ceiling using lengths of fine chain.

Stamp duty

Sometimes plain walls need more than a few pictures to liven them up, but if you can't face grappling with wallpaper, try stamping. With this nifty paint effect, you can cover a large area in a flash, adding as few or as many motifs as you like. You'll find a wide range of rubber stamps in art, craft and DIY stores, which should also sell the tiny roller you need to apply the paint to the stamp. You can buy special stamp paints, but undiluted emulsion is fine for walls and ceilings – sample pots go a long way.

1 Clean the wall using a soft scrubbing brush, and dry with a soft cloth. Pour a small amount of paint onto an old plate. Push the roller through the paint, then roll it over the raised surface of the stamp in a thin, even coat. Avoid applying too much as the stamp may smudge, or too little as the resulting image may be patchy. If paint seeps off the edge of the raised motif, clean it up with a cotton wool bud.

2 Carefully press the stamp face down onto the wall. To make sure you get even coverage, gently rock the stamp in all directions, taking care not to smudge the design. Lift the stamp away. If you make a mistake while stamping, wipe away wet paint with a clean damp cloth. If the print doesn't come out completely the first time, fill in details using a small artist's brush. Be sure to wash and dry your stamp between each application.

TIP
For a co-ordinated look, try stamping lampshades and cushion fabrics with the same design using fabric paint.

Little gems

Just a few handmade or designer tiles can make an amazing difference to a wallful of plain standard-issue ones, and making them yourself guarantees a unique look. These glittering tiles will add an air of glamour to any bathroom. They are created by casting plaster in a simple home-made mould and are set with a mix of sparkling glass beads and ordinary pebbles. Choose beads in colours that complement your room scheme, and pick up pebbles from your garden for a truly personal touch.

1 To make a mould, cut four 17cm lengths of 4 × 2cm wooden batten. Place them on 3mm-thick flexible board to make a 4cm-high box. Firmly fix the outer corners with masking tape.

2 Following the manufacturer's instructions, mix some plaster and pour into the mould as it thickens. Place a selection of pebbles and beads on top, arranging them in a circle. Leave the plaster until it has set, then take off the battens and flex the board to dislodge the tile.

3 Dot a few of the finished tiles at random among a wall of plain white ones or use them to make a border or basin splashback – you don't need many to add instant glamour.

Panel games

If you've ever fancied a wood-panelled 'library' effect in a sitting room or study, it's easy to create the look with a few pieces of wood. MDF planks up to about 15cm wide can simply be glued to the wall to form a grid and, when painted to blend in with the background colour, they create the illusion of period-style panelling. For a more informal panelled effect, glue just a few planks to the lower part of a wall. This is a good way of adding interest to a boring hallway and protects the walls from the wear and tear of daily traffic. The planks in the inset picture are made of softwood and tinted with woodstain.

1 Measure your wall and decide on the height and width of the panels. Remember to allow for the fact that you need to end with a plank of wood along each edge of the wall. Using a spirit level and a pencil, mark the positions of the horizontal planks on the wall, so that you get each piece of timber straight. Mark the positions for the vertical planks using a plumbline, again to help you get them straight.

2 Cut 4mm-thick MDF planks to size and glue them to the wall using strong wood adhesive. When the glue has dried, paint the entire wall with two coats of emulsion.

TIP
Stick your panelling onto a lined wall and it will be easy to remove if you want to change the look.

Square deal

Walls covered in checks can add pattern and pace to a room, but they may also overpower a small space if the contrast between the colours used is too great. If you like the look but want to avoid making your room look like a chess-board, try a more subtle approach. Using two similar shades creates a less garish effect, while choosing gloss emulsion for one and matt for the other creates a variation in texture as well as tone. Blue is a perfect colour to choose for this as its different shades blend harmoniously together.

1 Paint the whole of the wall using the lighter paint shade in matt emulsion. When this is dry, lightly mark out squares on your wall using a pencil and ruler, enlisting the help of a spirit level and plumbline to help you get the lines straight.

2 Mask off alternate squares using low-tack masking tape and paint these in a slightly darker shade of gloss emulsion. When the paint is dry, carefully peel away the tape. Check for any stray pencil marks and remove these using a soft rubber.

Climbing plants

A rambling stencil in a soft colour applied over a neutral base gives the look of expensive handpainted wallpaper. To cover a wall, you will need a repeat stencil, which is designed to create a seamless look. Buy a pre-cut stencil; if you choose a less intricate design the stencil company may offer a cheaper one you can cut out yourself, but if you're decorating a large area it's worth paying for a ready-cut version. For an even finish, use a tiny sponge roller instead of a brush to paint the design.

1 Make sure your wall is flat and free of cracks and blemishes. Paint the wall with emulsion in a light neutral shade and leave to dry.

2 Cover the back of the stencil with repositional spray adhesive, which allows it to

be moved and adjusted easily. Position it in a top corner of the wall, checking that it is straight. Pour some coloured emulsion onto an old plate and cover the sponge roller with paint, taking care not to overload it. Pass the roller over the stencil, pressing firmly and evenly until all details of the design are covered with paint.

3 Lightly mark a pencil dot in each of the registration holes on the stencil to ensure that the next design aligns exactly. Move the stencil to the next position and repeat the process until the wall has been covered.

TIP
It's a good idea to cover your wall with lining paper before painting to create a perfectly smooth surface for stencilling.

Silver lining

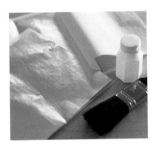

Take a shine to metal leaf and you'll see just how easy it can be to glam up walls and accessories. Great for adding a touch of glitz around your home, metal leaf is sold as fine sheets of gold or silver attached to a backing sheet. Cheaper versions of less precious metals are also available and look equally as stunning. These silvery squares, for example, are created using aluminium leaf. To apply the leaf, you will need a special glue called size and a soft brush to smooth it in place. It's best to use gold and

silver effects in moderation as overdoing them can look tacky rather than terrific. A couple of columns of silver squares used to highlight the wall near a dining area can enrich a whole room.

1 Use a ruler and pencil to mark the lines of the design on the wall, then mask off each of the squares using low-tack masking tape.

2 Brush a little metal size onto one of the squares on the wall and wait for it to become tacky, which should take about 15 minutes. Lay a sheet of metal leaf over the square and gently smooth it in place using a flat, soft brush, then remove the backing. Repeat for the remaining squares. Leave until the size is completely dry, before carefully peeling away the masking tape.

Screen play

Basin splashbacks might have a practical job to do but they don't need to be boring with it. So brighten up your bathroom and give yourself something to look at while cleaning your teeth. You don't need fancy designer tiles – the cut-price way to add colour and pattern is simply to take a piece of your favourite fabric and trap it behind a sheet of see-through acrylic. Sealing the edges ensures that the fabric stays dry.

1 Clear acrylic sheets are available from DIY stores – measure the area you want to cover and ask if you can have a piece cut to your exact size. Cut a piece of fabric to match the size of your acrylic panel, taking into account the positioning of any large designs or patterns.

2 Sandwiching the fabric between the wall and the acrylic sheet, fix the panel in place using mirror-head screws. Seal around the edges with clear bathroom sealant to prevent water from seeping in and soaking the fabric.

Wrapper's delight

Give plain ceramic vases an unusual textural covering using fine cotton cord. Winding it carefully around and gluing it in place creates an attractive ribbed surface. For a more rustic look, try using seagrass, jute or twine. Choose vases with simple shapes and smooth curves.

1 Mask the exterior of the vase with newspaper, then paint the inside and the rim using fast-drying enamel spray paint in a colour that contrasts with your cord. Apply it in several fine layers, leaving it to dry between coats. When the final layer is dry, remove the newspaper.

TIP
Don't pull the cord too tight when winding as this could cause gaps to appear between the coils.

2 Coat the lower half of the vase with adhesive and leave until tacky. Use a glue that stays tacky for a while before drying, such as impact or heavy-duty spray adhesive. Fasten the end of the cord at the base of the vase using masking tape. Keeping the vase upright, carefully wind the cord around it, making sure each loop sits snugly against the last. When you have covered the lower half, apply adhesive to the upper half and continue winding.

3 When you are 1cm from the top of the vase, apply a little extra adhesive to the remainder to ensure that the last coils of cord are secure. When you reach the top, cut diagonally across the cord, dab a little PVA adhesive onto the end of it and stick in place. Leave the glue to harden, then remove the masking tape. Using a soft brush, coat the cord with PVA diluted with an equal quantity of water, which acts as a seal.

Paper work

Papier-mâché is the simple craft used to conjure up this beautiful bowl. It's a technique we've all tried as kids using soggy strips of newspaper, but when you replace this with delicate handmade paper, and throw in a few leaves and a spot or two of silver leaf, the results are worthy of a designer's studio. Look for textured paper that is fine enough to let the leaves and silver show through. You will also need wallpaper paste, a glass bowl to use as a mould and some clingfilm to prevent the papier-mâché from sticking to the bowl.

1 Lay newspaper over your work surface, then prepare wallpaper paste following the packet instructions. Cover the outside of the glass bowl with clingfilm.

2 Tear handmade paper into strips. Coat each with paste by dipping it in then running it through your fingers to remove any excess. Smooth the strip onto the bowl. Repeat until the bowl is covered with paper. Leave to dry.

3 When the paper is dry, place the leaves on the bowl and apply a second layer of pasted paper over the top to hold them in place. Leave to dry.

4 Add patches of silver leaf by brushing a small amount of paste onto the bowl before carefully sticking the leaf in place. Add more layers of handmade paper until you are satisfied. When dry, separate the papier-mâché from the bowl by gently easing off the clingfilm. If splits appear, patch them with paste-coated paper.

TIP
Make sure each layer of papier-mâché is thoroughly dry before applying the next. A blast with a hairdryer will help to speed things up.

Feather report

Transform glass vases from plain to exquisite with delicate images derived from real feathers. You will need access to a colour photocopier, some wet release transfer paper and a collection of feathers.

1 Make colour photocopies of feathers onto the glossy side of the transfer paper, at a size appropriate for the vase. Fit as many feather images as you can onto the paper, either by using the copier's stop and repeat option or by copying the feathers onto plain paper first, then recopying onto the transfer sheet.

2 Cut carefully around the feather images. Submerge each in a bowl of lukewarm water and soak for a couple of minutes until the transfer images separate easily from the backing sheet. While the images are soaking, make sure your vase is clean and lightly wet it with cold water.

3 Carefully lift the feather transfer images out of the water (leaving the backing sheet behind) and place on the wetted vase. Gently slide the transfers around the vase until you find the position you want, smoothing out wrinkles or air bubbles with a finger or sponge. Dab gently with kitchen paper to remove excess water.

4 Leave the vase to dry for at least an hour before handling (a hairdryer can speed things up). If your vase is likely to come into regular contact with water, spray the decoration with a light coat of polyurethane varnish to waterproof it and prevent peeling or scratching.

TIP
If you prefer, use leaves or flowers instead of feathers. When copying, protect the copier surface from pollen by placing clear acetate underneath the flowers and white paper on top.

Shell out

1 Grate or slice some glycerine soap compound into thin slivers and heat gently, using a heatproof bowl over a pan of boiling water, just as you would for melting chocolate. Be very careful not to overheat the melted soap, as it can catch fire if left unattended.

Set your seashore treasures in the centre of home-made glycerine soaps and wait to see what gets washed up in your bath. Ideal for giving as gifts, these soaps are made by melting glycerine soap compound, available from craft shops, and then pouring it into a mould. For this, use any suitable container you may find around the house – cut-down drinks cartons are ideal. You can colour the soaps in the shade of your choice and also add essential oils to give them fragrance.

2 Add colour if you like, using soap colour blocks. Their colouring is very intense: this blue was achieved using only a pea-sized lump for two blocks of soap compound. Add the colour very gradually and mix in well before adding more. At this stage you can also add a few drops of essential oil for fragrance.

3 Pour 1cm or so of the mixture into a mould and leave for five to six minutes until almost set. Press your shell gently into it, and top up with melted soap compound until the shell is covered. Leave to set, then remove from the mould.

TIP
If you can't get to a beach to pick up shells, they are widely available in stores. Be sure to buy ones that come from properly managed sustainable sources.

Metallic markers

Make a set of trendy markers to keep tabs on pots of herbs. These shiny metallic leaves and flowers are cut from fine aluminium foil, and the embossed names and other details are simply drawn on using ballpoint pen. Add to the metallic look by displaying your plants in galvanized pots, then line them up along a shelf or windowsill.

1 Draw leaf and flower shapes on card and cut out to make templates. Lay the templates on 36-gauge aluminium foil and draw around them with ballpoint pen. Cut out the metal shapes using small sharp scissors.

2 Use an empty ballpoint pen to add markings on the petals and veins on the leaves. Write a plant name on the back of each marker, writing in reverse to create an embossed effect on the front. To transfer words in reverse to the back of foil, write them first on tracing paper, then place the tracing face down on the foil and re-draw over the lines. Glue each marker to a length of heavy galvanized wire.

Top of the pots

Terracotta pots cost very little at garden centres and DIY stores but can be transformed from bog-standard to beautiful with just a few coats of paint. These colourful planters boast a bold design that contrasts deep blue and white in vertical stripes, which are easy to create by using masking tape. If you feel more artistic, you could try making up your own designs.

1 Make sure your pot is clean and dry, then apply undercoat and allow to dry completely. This helps the paint colour stay true as terracotta pots are quite porous. Then paint on a coat of white emulsion and leave to dry.

2 To make the stripes, cut strips of masking tape and stick them carefully down the length of the pot, making sure they are totally flat. Paint over the whole pot again in the contrasting colour of your choice. When this second coat is dry, carefully remove the tape, and apply a coat of acrylic matt varnish to protect the paintwork.

Tray chic

Serve up breakfast in bed on a colourful mosaic-decorated tray. A mixed bag of individual tiles in pretty shades of blue turns a plain base into a real wake-up call, while the rest of the tray is painted in pure white. If possible, choose a tray made from unfinished wood, which can be painted without any preparation. These are available from companies that sell 'blanks', basic wooden accessories and furniture sold ready to paint.

1 Sand the base of the tray, then prime with a half-and-half mixture of PVA adhesive and water. Take enough mosaic tiles to cover your tray. Using a small brush, apply a blob of PVA to the rippled side of a tile, then stick in place on the base. Repeat until the area is covered, making sure you leave a gap between each tile for grout. Leave to dry overnight.

2 Mix some grout following the manufacturer's instructions. Using a squeegee, cover the tiles with grout, pressing it into the gaps and wiping off any excess with a damp sponge. When the grout is dry to the touch, polish the tiles with a soft cloth. Paint the rest of the tray with matt emulsion, followed by a couple of coats of acrylic varnish, leaving each coat to dry before applying the next.

Patio partners

Add the finishing touch to a trendy garden deck with some smart designer-style planters. These cool customers show off fresh white paintwork and borders of bright blue mosaic, but they started out as common-or-garden terracotta pots. With white gravel to complete the picture, they now have a slick contemporary look. If your patio is more traditional in style, you may prefer to paint the pots in blues or greens that blend in with your garden.

1 Thoroughly clean a large terracotta pot, then apply two coats of white floor paint, continuing it over the inside of the top rim. Leave each coat to dry.

2 Buy mosaic tiles that come attached to a backing sheet and cut a strip, two tiles wide, to fit around the rim of the

pot. Spread waterproof tile adhesive over the rim and stick on the mosaics, wavy side down, leaving the paper backing attached. Leave to set according to the manufacturer's instructions. When set, dampen the backing paper with a wet sponge and peel it off. Apply waterproof grout over the tiles, using a squeegee or sponge to push it into the gaps between them.

3 Put in your compost and plant, then sprinkle white gravel over the top of the compost.

Spud craft

You may think potato prints are just child's play, but they can create some slick designs on grown-up stationery. Simply cut your spuds into simple shapes, such as hearts or circles, and then stamp away. These designs are painted using nail polish, so search your make-up drawer for all those rather-too-shocking pinks and oranges that you no longer wear and put them to good use.

1 Cut a potato in half and use a craft knife to outline a simple shape on the cut surface of each half. Cut away the potato from around the shape so that it creates a raised stamp. Dry the potato with kitchen paper.

2 Coat the cut shapes lightly with nail polish, then press them onto notepaper. Reapply the nail polish before stamping each new motif.

Blues band

You don't need expensive vases to show off fresh flowers. Simply recycle a few shapely bottles from your kitchen cupboards, place one or two flower stems in each and group them together. Clear glass bottles look good without any further decoration, but if you want to give your display a colour boost, try painting them in different tones of the same hue. Spray paints make it easy to achieve even coverage.

1 Clean and thoroughly dry a used vinaigrette or wine bottle. Working in a well-ventilated area, place the bottle in an open cardboard box and spray it with an even coat of enamel paint, making sure you keep the spray contained in the box.

2 Paint more bottles of varying sizes in different tones of the same colour, then arrange them in a group together to make a stylish display.

Sew pretty

Add a special touch to a plain washbag with decorative embroidered flowers. Two simple stitches – chain and satin – are used to create a row of motifs. Before you start on the actual item, practise your stitching on a scrap of fabric.

1 Copy the outline of this simple flower design onto tracing paper and pin it, tracing side up, to the washbag. Slip dressmaker's carbon paper under the tracing, carbon side down, and softly pencil over the design lines. Repeat until you have transferred a row of flower designs to the bag.

2 Thread a sharp embroidery needle – crewel size 7 is ideal – with two strands of six-stranded embroidery cotton in pink. Embroider the petals using satin stitch: starting at one end of the area to be stitched, secure the thread

with backstitch then, inserting the needle just outside the marked lines, work parallel stitches close together to fill in the shape. Fasten off the thread at the back.

3 Using two strands of silver thread, satin stitch the leaves, then work a small dot in the centre of the petals. Add the stems in chain stitch: bring the needle up from the back of the fabric and reinsert it just beside the point at which it emerged. Bring the point of the needle out a small distance away and loop the thread under the point of the needle. Pull the needle through. Repeat to form the next loop in the chain.

TIP
If you want to work the design on a piece of fabric rather than a washbag, mounting it in a small embroidery hoop will make the sewing easier.

Gold plate

Give a trio of ordinary glass plates the Midas touch and make a glamorous display for your mantelpiece. The underside of each plate is decorated with gold leaf, applied to create simple geometric designs, and some of the clear areas have been given a frosted look with etching spray. Metallic gold leaf is sold in sheets, and you can also buy it in a kit which includes the other special items you need: size (the glue used for gilding), shellac varnish and brushes

1 Using masking tape, mark out your chosen pattern on the underside of the plate, covering the areas you don't want to gild. Using a brush, apply a thin layer of size over the rest of the underside and leave until the size becomes tacky to the touch.

2 Carefully lay a sheet of gold leaf onto the tacky surface and use a soft flat brush to gently stroke the foil in place. Continue applying sheets until the underside of the plate is covered. Leave to dry, then remove the tape and brush away any excess leaf before buffing with a soft cloth.

3 If you want to give the non-gilded areas of your plate a frosted look, spray the back of the plate with a thin coat of etching spray. When this is dry, add a coat of shellac varnish to seal the decoration.

TIP
If the gold leaf breaks up slightly while you are applying it, don't panic. This will only add to the handcrafted effect and texture of the decoration.

Scent sensation

These tiny sachets slip easily into a drawer or wardrobe to fill your clothes with the fresh scent of lavender. Taking just minutes to make, they would also be great as last-minute stocking fillers for Christmas. Wide ribbon is used for the body of the bag – gather together a mixture of plain and striped ribbons to create a varied selection of sachets.

1 Using ribbon of at least 5cm wide, cut a piece approximately 30cm long. Hem the raw ends, then fold the ribbon in half with right sides facing so that the hemmed ends meet. Stitch down both sides, close to the edge, then turn the bag right side out.

2 Fill the sachet with dried lavender and tie at the neck with narrow ribbon. If you want to hang the sachet in a wardrobe, tie the ends of the narrow ribbon together to make a loop.

Rustic charm

Treat a battered old tray to a facelift by covering it with hessian fabric. This woven material has a rough natural texture, which is perfect for injecting a hint of homely country style into a kitchen. The look is completed by wrapping the handles of the tray with parcel string.

1 Remove the handles of the tray. Cut a rectangle of hessian to cover its inner surface and edges. Cut another rectangle to fit over the base, outer edges and top edges of the tray, allowing 1cm extra all round.

2 Using fabric adhesive, glue the outer piece of hessian in place over the base and edges, continuing the 1cm excess down over the inside edges. Snip into the fabric at the corners and mitre it neatly. Glue the other piece of fabric to the inside surface and edges, lapping it over the first piece of hessian at the top of the inner edges.

3 To seal the hessian, dilute one part PVA adhesive with five parts water and brush it over the whole of the tray. Hold the fabric in place with clothes pegs while it dries, then trim any excess fabric at the top edges. Bind the handles with brown parcel string, then replace them on the tray.

Bejewelled

Turn plain tableware into pieces that look as if they've just popped out of a treasure chest. Glowing cabochons (shiny glass beads) can be used to glam up the borders of plates or the rims of bowls. Although the decorated items might not stand up to the rigours of everyday wear and tear, they would be great for adding a bit of extra sparkle to a special-occasion meal. This frosted glass platter and bowl, jazzed up with gold cabochons, team up to make a showy table centrepiece.

1 Take a plain ceramic or glass plate. Stick your coloured glass cabochons around its perimeter using epoxy resin, arranging them in a pleasingly random design.

2 Take a bowl that matches the plate. (It needs to have a chunky rim that is flat at the top.) Stick a few more of the glass cabochons around the rim. Fill the bowl with small, colourful fruits or foil-wrapped sweets and place it in the centre of the plate to make a display for a table or sideboard.

Flower power

Give a plain glass plate a bright, summery look with colourful flower motifs. Giftwrap is a good source of motifs, or you could cut some from old magazines or books. The flowers are simply pasted face down onto the underside of a clear plate, so that they can be seen through the glass from above, and the white background is added with enamel paint. The matching vase is decorated in the same way, on the inside – remember to choose one that's large enough to allow you to get your hand in. After decorating, the glassware can be washed carefully but not soaked in water.

1 Take a clear glass plate and vase, wash in detergent and leave to dry. Using sharp scissors, carefully cut out paper flower motifs and position them evenly around the underside of the plate. Using paper glue, stick the motifs in place by brushing the glue onto the plate and pressing each flower in place. Smooth from centre to edges to remove air bubbles and wipe off excess glue with a damp sponge.

2 When the glue is dry, brush on a coat of clear acrylic varnish to seal. Leave to dry, then apply two or three coats of enamel paint in your chosen colour all over the underside of the plate.

3 Stick more flower motifs on the inside of the vase. Seal them with varnish, then apply the enamel paint on the inside also, as for the plate.

TIP
As the vase is decorated on the inside you will need to place another glass jar inside if you want to use it for fresh flowers.

Designs on china

Ever thought of creating your own designs for tableware? Plain white china provides a blank canvas for painting, and it's easy if you stick to simple, geometric designs such as small blocks, stripes and dots of colour. Ceramic paints that can be hardened in the oven create a durable finish on china – just check that the ones you buy are safe to eat off once fixed. Try decorating a few plates and then, if you like the results, why not go on to tackle a complete dinner service? On smaller pieces, such as cups and saucers, use a narrow brush to form fine bands of colour.

1 Wash each plate in warm soapy water to remove grease, and dry thoroughly.

2 Using a soft flat artist's brush, paint a border of blocks about 2cm wide all around the rim of each plate. If you want a regular design, mark it out first using a chinagraph pencil. If you make mistakes, you can wipe off the paint before it dries. When you've painted on all the blocks, leave to dry.

3 Use a nail or craft knife to scratch horizontal lines into the dry paint so that the white shows through. When you're happy with the design, bake the plate in the oven to fix the paint, carefully following the manufacturer's instructions.

Weighty matters

Clip this elegant ornamental weight to the corner of your tablecloth to keep it in place. It comes in especially handy if you're eating outdoors on a breezy day, and makes an attractive finishing touch at any time. Mix a selection of coloured beads with metallics for a high-glamour look. You'll find a wide range of beads available, but it's fun to buy some plain glass ones and paint them with your own choice of colours and designs. Check out your local craft shop for paints and outliner pens suitable for use on glass.

1 Wrap masking tape around one end of a cocktail stick and push a bead onto it so it is secure enough not to slip off. Repeat for other beads. Holding the stick, dip each bead into a bottle of glass paint. Shake surplus paint back into the bottle, then sit the sticks in Blu-Tack until the paint has dried.

2 Use an outliner pen to draw designs on the beads in contrasting colours. When the paint is dry, remove the beads from the sticks and thread them onto a 10cm length of jewellery wire attached to the base of a curtain clip. Use pliers to cut the wire ends, and push the ends into the bead centres to hide them. Hang from the corner of any tablecloth.

TIP
If you don't have any Blu-Tack to hand, push the cocktail sticks into half a potato instead while the beads are drying.

Reflected glory

The flickering flame of a tealight casts glowing reflections in the mirrored walls of this smart contemporary candle sconce. The simple design is easy to put together using three pieces of MDF, which are then covered with mirror mosaic tiles. These are the easiest of mosaics to work with, as they need no grouting. Buy tiles sold in sheets, attached to backing paper, so that you don't have to stick them on individually.

1 From 2cm-thick MDF, cut three pieces: one of 10cm square, another of 12cm square and the third measuring 10 × 12cm. Place them together to make the sconce and glue the edges using woodworking adhesive. Seal the MDF with a mixture of half PVA adhesive and half water. Leave to dry.

2 From a sheet of paper-backed mirror mosaic tiles, cut three 10cm squares to cover the inner surfaces of the sconce and three 12cm squares to cover the outer surfaces. Cut strips one tile wide to cover the edges. To fix the mosaics to the sconce, squeeze PVA glue onto the tiled side of the square or strip and place in position. When the sconce is covered, leave for about four hours until the glue is dry. To remove the backing paper, dampen it with a sponge and leave for several minutes, then gently peel away.

Cracking idea

Twinkling candlelight enhances the romance of summer evenings, so have some illuminations on hand to bring some magic to your outdoor table. If you don't want to bring out your best candleholders, try this original idea using an eggbox and half a dozen eggshells. The shells are filled with candle sand, a material made from tiny beads of wax, which allows you to turn almost any non-flammable receptacles into candles. The candle sand is sold complete with a selection of wicks.

1 Break the tops of six eggs and remove the contents, making sure that the main part of the shell remains intact. Wash out the shells and leave to dry, then place them in a cardboard eggbox.

2 Carefully fill each shell about half full with candle sand. Insert wicks in the sand and light.

It's a snip

The organic shapes on this lampshade are simply pieces of paper, pasted onto its plain yellow background. The dark areas are created by using a double layer, and here and there you can cut sections out so light shines through.

1 Remove a plain paper lampshade from its base, then locate the seam and position it on a large piece of paper. Mark the paper at the top and bottom of the seam and join the two marks with a straight pencil line. Slowly roll the shade across the paper, drawing along the top and bottom edges as you go, until you come to the seam again. You will end up with the outline of your lampshade drawn on paper.

2 Draw your design on this template, shading areas according to how light or dark you want them. When you're happy with your design, outline the shapes on tracing paper.

3 Transfer the shapes to white and yellow A4 paper. Using sharp scissors or a craft knife, cut them out. Rub off any pencil marks that might show when light shines through.

4 Pour PVA adhesive into a saucer and, using a brush, apply a thin layer to the backs of the paper shapes. Press them onto the shade, adding extra layers of paper to areas you want to look darker. Allow the glue to dry thoroughly before cutting sections out with a very sharp craft knife. Apply several coats of clear polyurethane spray varnish. When dry, fit the shade onto your lamp.

TIP
When cutting out sections from the shade, protect your fingers by taping a thick piece of corrugated card inside the shade underneath the area you are cutting.

Hot metal

Create this gorgeous lamp by attaching bands of leaf shapes cut from aluminium foil to a shade made from metal mesh.

1 Make a lampshade template by drawing two semi-circles, 27cm apart, on paper. The top edge of the shade should measure 56cm, the bottom 68cm. Measure these distances along the arcs and join with a straight line. Cut out the shape. Draw around the template on fine metal mesh and cut out. Join the straight edges with short lengths of fine wire: double them over and poke them through the mesh, then twist ends together with pliers.

2 Push a 20cm-diameter utility ring into base of shade, then attach it to the mesh with fine wire. Make a 17cm-diameter circle of heavy galvanized wire to fit 1cm below top of shade and wire it into place. Fold 1cm mesh at top over to inside of the shade.

3 Draw a leaf shape, 8cm high, 7cm wide, on thin card, and cut out. Place on 36-gauge aluminium foil and draw around it. Repeat to make a band of leaves to fit the shade and cut it out using small scissors. Draw veins on the back of the leaves with a ballpoint pen. Using a pair of compasses, pierce two holes 1cm from straight edge, between each leaf. Attach to shade with fine wire through holes. Cover shade with more bands. To neaten top of shade, fold a 3cm-wide strip of foil over edge.

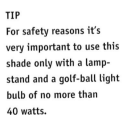

TIP
For safety reasons it's very important to use this shade only with a lamp-stand and a golf-ball light bulb of no more than 40 watts.

All the trimmings

Candy stripes of ribbon in two contrasting colours form a pretty decoration for a plain white lampshade, with braid adding a finishing touch around the top and bottom edges. Pastel colours and flowers would be ideal for a feminine bedroom. There is a wide range of ribbons to choose from so this idea could very easily be adapted to suit any room scheme.

1 Measure around the top and bottom rims of your lampshade and lightly pencil eight evenly spaced vertical lines down the shade. Measure the length of the shade and cut pieces of narrow ribbon to size, adding 3cm (to give a 1cm overlap at the top and a 2cm overlap at the bottom).

2 Stick double-sided tape to the back of the ribbon and stick to the shade to cover the pencil lines. Stick the overlaps to the inside of the shade at top and bottom. Measure equal distances between the narrow ribbons and stick lengths of wider contrasting ribbon in place at these points.

3 Cut lengths of braid to fit around the top and bottom rims of the shade, adding 2cm to each length. Fix the braid in place using a glue gun or strong fabric glue, overlapping the ends to give a neat finish.

Cut-price chandelier

If you love the luxurious look of glittering chandeliers but not their price tags, then re-create that essential sparkle with glass beads dangling from a pendant light fitting. You will need a selection of beads in different sizes and shapes: small ones to go around the pendant ring and a mix of long beads and large round ones for the drops.

1 Decorate a 15cm-diameter pendant ring with two coats of enamel paint, then one coat of clear enamel varnish, allowing it to dry between coats. Cut a 70cm length of jewellery wire and thread on the first small bead. Fold over the end of the wire and twist it with small round-nosed pliers (or jewellery pliers), then continue threading on small beads until there is just 1cm of wire remaining. Fold this over the last bead and twist the wire to secure the beads. Wrap the beaded wire around the ring.

2 To make the bead drops, cut assorted lengths of wire and thread on a selection of glass beads, starting with the heaviest and securing the ends of the wire by twisting it as before. Leave about 2.5cm of wire free to secure the drop to the ring.

3 Secure the first bead drop by wrapping the free end of wire tightly around the ring. Repeat this process to make and attach drops evenly as before. Remove the bulb from the light fitting, slip the ring over, then refit the bulb. Do not use the shade with a light bulb of more than 40 watts.

Fringe benefits

Natural materials such as wood and stone are great for adding a touch of warmth and texture to modern rooms decorated in plain neutral colours. Natural fabrics have the same effect, so try giving a sleek modern lamp a more laid-back look by wrapping the shade in a length of raffia matting. Matching fringing conceals the raw edges around the top and bottom and adds further textural interest.

1 Remove the lampshade and measure its height and circumference, adding 2cm to each measurement. Cut a piece of raffia matting to this size. Apply fabric glue to both the matting and the shade. Starting at one edge of the matting, roll it onto the shade. Trim away excess matting and make sure the overlap seam is glued securely.

2 To finish cut lengths of raffia fringing to fit around the top and bottom of the shade. Glue in place, positioning as shown in the picture opposite.

TIP
Lampshades can be covered in many different types of fabrics, to suit your style. If you like a more sumptuous look, check out remnant boxes for offcuts of luxurious, expensive materials.

Plastic fantastic

Make a lamp that doubles as a picture and displays your favourite items behind a sheet of laminated plastic. Choose flat objects, such as feathers or leaves, plus a piece of handmade paper to act as an attractive background. The laminating is carried out by pressing the items with an iron between pieces of clear PVC plastic sheeting. Clipping a light bracket behind the plastic turns your picture into an unusual wall lamp.

1 Select the items to be laminated and cut a sheet of handmade paper on which to arrange them. From a roll of PVC plastic sheeting, cut two identical pieces of PVC large enough to cover the paper, adding a border of at least 6cm all round. Place one PVC sheet on top of some baking paper, arrange the paper and items on top, and place the other PVC sheet over them, making a sandwich. Cover with a sheet of baking paper.

2 With a medium-hot iron, carefully press down onto the layers, making sure you cover all the PVC with the heat. You can peek to see if the plastic has bonded. Peel off the baking paper but take care – it will be hot. Allow to cool.

3 Using a bulldog clip, fix a light bracket behind the plastic and mount on the wall to make an unusual lamp. Use it with a light bulb of no more than 40 watts.

Rich glow

Make a lampbase look like a million dollars with a shimmering golden finish. Inexpensive metallic leaf can be applied using traditional gilding techniques, but gives the same glow as real gold for a fraction of the price. To make shopping for the ingredients easy, see if you can find a kit that includes everything you need: metallic gold leaf, size (glue for gilding), shellac varnish and brushes. Choose a lampbase that has a smooth surface.

1 Using a brush, apply a thin layer of size over the entire surface of the lampbase. Leave to dry until the size is tacky to the touch.

2 Carefully lay a sheet of gold leaf onto the tacky surface using a soft brush. Continue applying sheets until the whole of the base is covered. Don't worry too much if the sheets overlap slightly or if you need to fill in any gaps later, as this will actually enhance the overall effect. Leave to dry, then buff with a soft cloth before sealing with a coat of shellac varnish.

3 Mask off a row of squares all the way around the lampshade with masking tape. Apply a thin layer of size to each square. Carefully cut the gold leaf to roughly the same dimensions as your masked-off squares, then apply as before. Once the gold leaf is completely dry, remove the masking tape and gently rub away any excess loose leaf with a soft cloth. Do not seal the shade with shellac varnish.

TIP
Sheets of gilding foil are very fragile and usually separated by layers of tissue. To avoid damaging the foil, only remove them as you need them and keep the tissue in place until the last moment.

Twilight zone

Get your garden glowing on a warm night with soft, diffused light from these stylish lanterns. Fine copper mesh makes a perfect shade for candles and tealights and is easy to fold or bend into shape. Shiny paper fasteners add a smart finishing touch while holding the lantern edges together.

1 Cut a piece of mesh to the size required and neaten the edges by folding them over twice, as you would to sew a hem. Wrap the mesh around a cylindrical object such as a vase or glass to achieve the right shape, overlapping the edges.

2 Using a ruler, measure off marks for the paper fasteners along the overlap, and cut little slits at each of these points for the fasteners to slip into. These will keep the lantern in shape. If you like, try pleating the mesh to create a star effect. Place a tealight or candle inside each lantern.

Let it bead

A curtain made from strings of glass beads screens a window pane with droplets of sparkling colour as light filters through them. This is a good way of brightening up a dull window without blocking out light.

1 Using a fret saw, cut a length of dowelling rod slightly longer than the width of your window recess. Make pencil marks on the dowelling at 7cm intervals. Carefully drill a small hole through the dowelling at each pencil mark.

2 Arrange beads in rows – the number of rows should equal the number of holes in the dowelling. Create a random arrangement of colours and sizes, mixing longer beads with round ones and discs.

3 Cut waxed cotton to the length you want your curtain, plus extra for knots between the beads. Tie a knot at one end of the cotton, thread on a bead,

then knot on the other side to secure. Thread on the remaining beads in the row one by one, knotting the cotton before and after each bead and spacing them evenly. For the discs, wind the cotton through the hole and around the bead a couple of times. Repeat with the other rows of beads.

4 Thread the top of each bead string through a hole in the rod, then tie a knot at the top to secure and cut off any excess cotton. When you have attached all the bead strings to the rod, flex the dowelling and place in the window recess – it will be self-supporting.

TIP
When drilling holes through the dowelling you will find it easier if you fix the rod to the worktop with masking tape, or hold it steady using a small clamp. Take care not to drill through your work surface!

Keep tabs on it

A curtain with a tab-top gives a contemporary look. Either make a single curtain to pull across or, for a wider window, make a pair. You may need to join two pieces of fabric together to get the required width.

1 To find the curtain length measure the depth of your window and add 11.5cm. For the width, measure and add half again, plus 6cm. Stitch 1.5cm double hems on each side edge. Decide how far apart the tabs will be (12.5 to 15cm). For each, cut a 27 × 13cm fabric strip.

2 Fold each tab in half, right sides facing, and stitch 1.5cm from edges. Press seam open with toe of iron. Turn each tab to right side, fold so seam lies in the centre and press.

3 Fold each tab to bring raw edges together and pin to top edge of curtain. Space tabs evenly. Cut a fabric strip 10cm deep and the width of the curtain plus 3cm. Turn under 1.5cm on one long edge and stitch. Pin over the tabs, right side down, matching raw edge to curtain edge. Stitch strip to curtain, 1.5cm from raw edges, then fold away from curtain and press flat. Machine stitch close to seam to hold fabric flat. Fold this piece of fabric to back of curtain and press. Turn under 1.5cm at each short end and slipstitch to sides of curtain.

4 Hand or machine stitch a double 5cm hem on lower edge of curtain.

Spot the difference

A café curtain provides privacy during the day by screening the lower half of a window, but you may feel that the traditional gathered or lacy styles look too fussy when teamed with full-length drapes. For a sharper, space-age feel, make this neat blind by cutting a series of small circles from silvery foil and sticking them onto clear plastic. A simple voile curtain softens the look slightly and can be drawn across to give greater privacy at night.

1 Cut a panel of clear plastic to size. Cut circles from aluminium foil using small sharp scissors. To get perfect circles, draw around an object such as a tin or bottle. Glue the circles onto the plastic in evenly spaced rows.

2 To hang the blind, make holes along the top edge using a hole punch and insert small split rings. Thread a length of fine wire through the rings and fix it to hooks at either side of the window frame.

Rising sun

Based on a walk-through Japanese door panel, this design works just as well on a window. Dip-dyeing creates a graduated effect on the panels of the blind, while the top is decorated with tie-dyed circles.

1 For the top panel, cut a strip of cotton fabric 2cm wider than the window and about a third of the depth. For the lower panels, cut one piece to cover the rest of the window, adding 6cm to both length and width. Wash these pieces and some leftover fabric (to use for tabs). Leave damp.

2 Mark three equally spaced points along the top panel, pinch the points between your fingers and wrap tightly with string. Mix cold water dye according to the maker's instructions, then immerse the string-tied strip and tab fabric in the dye bath. Rinse, untie string, dry and press.

3 To dye the remaining fabric, peg it to a rod placed across two chairs. Immerse lower half into dye bath, then raise it 30cm or so every 20 minutes. Rinse, dry and press, then cut it into three equal panels. Stitch a 1cm hem on sides and base of each, and on side edges of top panel. Join lower panels to bottom edge of top panel, trim seam and zig-zag to neaten.

4 For tabs, cut 5 × 17cm strips, press 1cm to wrong side on both long edges of each, then fold in half lengthways with pressed edges inside and stitch close to edges. Follow step 3 on page 188 to finish.

TIP
Keep the Japanese theme going by hanging the blind from a bamboo pole. Support it using centre brackets, then decorate the pole ends with tassels.

Chain gang

This super-cool modern blind runs smoothly on silvery chains and eyelets. Choose a sheer fabric and buy fine nickel-plated chain five times the length of your window. Eyelets are available in a kit that includes the hole punch.

1 Cut fabric to the size of your window, adding 4cm to the width, 10cm to the length. Make a 1cm double hem on each side edge, and a 2.5cm double hem on bottom edge. Starting just above bottom hem, mark eyelet positions 10cm from side edges and 20cm apart. Fix eyelets following kit instructions.

2 Cut a 25 × 25cm batten to width of blind and drill a hole at each end. On underside of batten, fix one screw eye 10cm from each end and a third 2cm from end of the cleat (double hook). Using a staple gun, fix top edge of blind to top of batten, doubling fabric over for strength. Insert a 5mm steel rod through bottom hem and sew hem ends closed.

3 Starting at opposite side from cleat, and working from front of blind, thread the chain up through all the screw eyes on the batten. Allow enough chain to hang down on the cleat side of the blind as far as the cleat position, then double it back on itself, thread it through the two nearest screw eyes and down through remaining eyelets.

4 Fix a washer to each chain end, using pliers to prise open the links. Fix batten in place by screwing through holes into window frame. Fix cleat at hand height on the frame.

TIP
If you can't be bothered with sewing, use iron-on tape for the hems and you won't even have to pick up a needle.

On the wire

Make fun shapes from fine copper wire, then display them in see-through pockets stitched to a blind. Choose sheer fabrics, such as linen voile, for both the blind and pockets, so that the light shines through to show off the shapes. Use copper tubing as a pole, adding decorative finials made from the same wire.

1 Cut fabric to the size of your window, adding 6.5cm to the length and 2cm to the width. Stitch a 1cm hem on each side edge, and a 2.5cm double hem along the bottom edge of the fabric. To make and attach the tabs, cut 17cm squares of fabric, then follow instructions for steps 2 and 3 of the tab-top curtain on page 188.

2 To make the coloured pockets, cut rectangles from contrasting fabrics. Fray the edges, then pin the pockets at random to the blind. Using a crewel needle and contrasting embroidery silk, sew small running stitches 5mm from the side and bottom edges of each pocket.

3 Use pliers to bend 1mm copper wire into simple shapes to fit into the pockets – spirals, daisies and leaves are all easy. Fix 19mm centre brackets to the window frame. Slot a 15cm copper tube through the tabs and brackets, and then twirl copper wire around the tube ends to make finials. Slot a wire shape into each of the pockets.

TIP
To save on sewing you could use a ready-made muslin panel, then all you need to do is attach the pockets using simple running stitch.

Frosty outlook

If you want to screen a
small window without sewing
a stitch, take a look at the array
of beautiful handmade papers
available from stationers and
craft shops. With designs
and textures to equal the finest
fabrics, they can be glued onto
lengths of bamboo to make a
simple blind. To make the most
of the light, choose thin papers
in pale colours – the delicate
texture and fern design of this
one gives the look of a frosted
window pane.

1 Fit a cup hook at each side
of your window frame. Cut a
piece of bamboo long enough
to extend slightly past them.

2 Trim handmade paper to
fit the window, adding 5cm
to the length. Use double-sided
tape to stick the paper to the
pole, making sure it is centred
and hanging straight. Cut
more bamboo to the width
of the paper and, using the
tape, stick it to the base of the
blind to weigh it down.

Instant solutions

Tablecloths, napkins and even tea towels or sheets can all make excellent quick-fix window treatments. As they are already hemmed, there is no sewing required, and if you use pincer clips to hang them you don't need to worry about any fiddly headings either. The top of a tablecloth can be folded over to adjust it to the right length and make a decorative valance. Tea towels and napkins are the perfect size for making café curtain panels – simply position your pole according to their size so that they hang to meet the sill at the bottom.

1 To make a curtain, take a heavy linen tablecloth of the correct size to cover your window: for fullness it should be at least one-and-a-half times the width of the window. If you want a decorative valance, the cloth should be 20 to 30cm longer than the length of the window. Fold over the valance at the top, adjusting its depth so that the curtain hangs to the correct length, and press.

2 Fix curtain clips along the fold, spacing them equal distances apart. To hang the curtain, simply hook the clips onto the rings of a curtain pole.

Individual style

If you've got a plain roller blind that could do with livening up, an easy and very effective way to customize it is by inserting a decorative mat or table runner in the centre. Choose a mat with a design that complements the colour of your blind, so that the insert blends in well with its surroundings. If you prefer, you could use several smaller table mats or napkins rather than one large one, dotting them around at random over the blind.

1 Lay a plain roller blind out on a flat surface. Place a decorative mat in the centre so that it will be well positioned when the blind is down. Pin the mat in place, then machine or hand sew, close to its edges.

2 Carefully cut away the blind behind the mat, about 1cm away from the line of stitching.

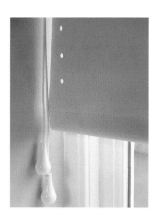

TIP
For an even simpler way of customizing a brightly coloured roller blind, try punching a row of holes down the sides.

Mirror magic

A plain curtain gets a retro look with oblong patches of felt that act as windows for small mirrors. This mimics the fashion for mirrored fabric effects and adds a reflective twinkle to your drapes as the mirrors catch the light. A glazier should be able to cut the pieces of mirror to size for you. Choose felt in a selection of different colours that harmonize tonally with your curtain fabric.

1 Get mirror offcuts cut to the size you want. From thin card, cut an oblong template 1cm larger all round than the mirrors, then use it to cut shapes from coloured felt.

2 Cut oval windows from the felt patches, then use matching embroidery thread to sew running stitch around the cut window edge, to prevent any stretching.

3 Stitch the felt patches at random to your curtain, sewing with embroidery thread and running stitch around their outer edges. Slip a mirror into each felt window before sewing the top edge.

Head start

The ruffled top on these elegant curtains is created using heading tape. Cords woven into it pull up to form pleats or gathers depending on the type used.

1 The tape instructions will say how wide the fabric must be to allow for gathering. Cut fabric to required size, adding 20cm to the length for hems and heading. Make double 1.5cm hems down each side. Hem bottom edge by turning up 2cm then 8cm.

2 On top edge of curtain, press 10cm to wrong side and tack close to raw edge. Cut heading tape to width of curtain, plus 4cm. Position tape right side up and 8cm down from top edge so it hides raw heading edge and extends 2cm beyond each side. Pin in place. At leading edge of curtain, pull tape cords from wrong side of tape and knot together. Turn under 2cm of raw end of tape and pin.

3 On remaining end of heading tape, pull out cords and leave free. Tuck in 2cm of raw end of tape. Stitch heading tape in place along top and lower edges, working in the same direction each time to stop any puckering.

4 Pull up loose cord ends to gather curtain to half the window's width. Loosely knot cord ends to secure. Make sure gathers are even, then insert hooks into pockets in the tape, spacing them 10cm apart. Wind loose cord into a bundle and secure with a few stitches. Don't cut off the excess.

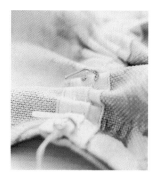

TIP
Sew velvet ribbon along the top and leading edges of your curtains to add a graceful finishing touch.

Spring blooms

Give a window a fresh look for spring by making a simple white voile panel scattered with pretty blue flowers. The blooms are fixed to the fabric using an iron-on bonding material (such as Bondaweb), which offers a quick no-sew method of fusing one fabric to another using an iron.

1 Cut a piece of linen voile to the size of your window, adding 4cm to the width and 14cm to the length for hems. Make 1cm double hems down the side edges. Turn up 2cm then 5cm along the top and bottom edges, then machine stitch.

2 To make the flowers, take a fabric in a contrasting colour.

Following the manufacturer's instructions, lay Bondaweb on the wrong side of this fabric and press. Draw a flower design on card and cut it out to make a template. Using this, draw flower shapes on the Bondaweb backing, then cut out.

3 Lay the voile on a flat surface and arrange the flower shapes on top. When they are positioned as you want, remove the Bondaweb backing. Cover the shapes with a damp cloth and press to fix them.

4 To hang the panel, fix pincer clips and rings along its top edge and thread the rings onto a pole.

STOCKISTS:

ART AND CRAFT EQUIPMENT

AZURRA
Suppliers of coloured glass mosaic tiles available by mail order (similar to those used for the mosaic mirror project on page 8, the mosaic tray on page 142 and the mosaic flowerpots on page 144).
Tel: 0845 090 8110
www.mosaics.co.uk

BRAMWELLS
Stoskists of of appliqué glue and appliqué foil (as used for the table runner project on page 77).
Tel: 01282 860388

CANDLE MAKERS SUPPLIES
Suppliers of batik wax and tools (as used for the batik cushion cover project on page 57).
Tel: 020 7602 4031

CREATIVE BEADCRAFT
Specialist company offering a wide range of beads, sequins and trimmings available by mail order.
Tel: 01494 778818
www.creativebeadcraft.co.uk

DYLON
Manufacturers of fabric dyes in a good range of colours, suitable for both washing machine and hand use (as used for the tie-dyed box cover on page 42, the dyed raffia mat on page 80, the tie-dyed tablecloth on page 83 and the dip-dyed curtain project on page 192).
Tel: 020 8663 4296
www.dylon.co.uk

THE ENGLISH STAMP COMPANY
Suppliers of interior design stamps, specialist tools, paper and paints by mail order.
Tel: 01929 439117
www.englishstamp.com

HARVEY BAKER DESIGN
Wooden storage boxes and bins (as used for the drilled storage box project on page 54).
Tel: 01803 521515
www.harvey-baker-design.co.uk

HAWKIN & CO
Suppliers of candle sand (as used in the eggshell candles on page 168).
Tel: 01986 782536

HOMECRAFTS DIRECT
Wide range of craft products available by mail order.
Tel: 0116 269 7733
www.homecrafts.co.uk

HUMBROL
Makers of the Glass Etch spray for creating a frosted effect on glass or Perspex (as used for the etched mirror frame project on page 24 and the Perspex screen on page 114). Also makers of chrome paints (as used on the silver chair on page 91).
Tel: 01482 701191

L. CORNELISSEN & SON
Suppliers of a wide range of traditional artists' materials plus aluminium, silver and gold leaf and specialist tools for gilding.
Tel: 020 7636 1045
www.cornelissen.co.uk

LIBERON
Makers of gilt cream, waxes and wood finishes.
Tel: 01797 367555

LONDON GRAPHIC CENTRE
Specialist shop offering a range of design sundries, art and craft supplies plus a good selection of handmade papers.
Tel: 020 7759 4500
www.londongraphics.co.uk

THE MOSAIC WORKSHOP
Suppliers of mosaic tiles (as used for the mirror project on page 8, the tray on page 142, the flowerpots on page 144 and the mosaic candle sconce on page 166) plus specialist tools and supplies.
Tel: 020 7272 2446
www.mosaicworkshop.com

THE PAINTED FINISH
Suppliers of glazes, varnishes and tools for creating specialist paint effects.
Tel: 01926 842 376
www.craftychick.com

ART AND CRAFT EQUIPMENT

PAPERCHASE
Modern and design-conscious stationery retailers offering a good range of wrapping and tissue papers, ribbons, twines plus cardboard and plastic boxes and containers suitable for storage.
Tel: 020 7467 6200 for branches or 0161 839 1500 for mail order
www.paperchase.co.uk

PENTONVILLE RUBBER
Suppliers of foam rubber.
Tel: 020 7837 4582

PLASTI-KOTE
Makers of aerosol spray paints for decorative use, including glass-frosting spray, metallic finishes and sprays suitable for use with stencils.
Tel: 01223 836 400
www.spraypaint.co.uk

ROYAL SOVEREIGN
Makers of Wireform copper mesh (as used for the lanterns on page 185).
Tel: 020 8888 6888

SCUMBLE GOOSIE
Ready-to-paint furniture and accessories including blanks for screens, trays and lampbases.
Tel: 01453 731315
www.scumble-goosie.co.uk

SPECIALIST CRAFTS

Makers of a wide range of craft products.
Tel: 0116 269 7711 for stockists or 0116 269 7733 for mail order
www.speccrafts.co.uk

THE STENCIL LIBRARY

Stencils and stencilling tools by mail order.
Tel: 01661 844844
www.stencil-library.com

THE STENCIL STORE

A wide range of stencils and specialist paints available by mail order or from branches nationwide.
Tel: 01923 285577
www.stencilstore.com

VV ROULEAUX

Extraordinarily wide range of haberdashery including ribbons, braids, cords, trimmings, beads, sequins, feathers and curtain tassels.
Mail order available.
Tel: 020 7434 3899
www.vvrouleaux.com

WOOLWORTHS

Stockists of Dylon fabric dyes (see page 210) plus a small range of craft basics such as glues, paint brushes and paints.
Tel: 01706 862789
www.woolworths.co.uk

FABRICS

ALMA HOME
Leather and suede available in
a good range of colours.
Tel: 020 7377 0762
www.almahome.co.uk

BERWICK STREET CLOTH SHOP
Wide range of inexpensive
fabrics including felts and latex
plus a good selection of
brightly coloured cotton voiles.
Tel: 020 7287 2881

CALICO
Sells everything from voiles
and muslins to PVC-coated,
tapestry and furnishing fabrics.
Tel: 029 2049 3020

CATH KIDSTON
Romantic 1950s-style floral
prints with retro feel.
Tel: 020 7221 4000 for stockists
or 020 7229 8000 for mail order
www.cathkidston.co.uk

DESIGNER'S GUILD
Colourful and contemporary
fabric and soft furnishings.
Tel: 020 7351 5775
www.designersguild.com

DYLON
Manufacturers of fabric dyes in
a wide range of colours,
suitable for both washing
machine and hand use (as used
for the tie-dyed box cover on
page 42, the dyed raffia mat on
page 80, the tie-dyed tablecloth
on page 83 and the dip-dyed
curtain project on page 192).
Tel: 020 8663 4296
www.dylon.co.uk

JOHN LEWIS

Department store offering a wide selection of fabrics, haberdashery and curtain trimmings, including Rufflette (see page 220).
Tel: 020 7629 7711
www.johnlewis.co.uk

MALABAR

Hand-woven silks and cotton fabrics imported from India.
Tel: 020 7501 4200
www.malabar.co.uk

THE NATURAL FABRIC COMPANY

Wide range of natural fabrics, from hessian and calico to chambray and sheers.
Tel: 01488 684002

VV ROULEAUX

Extraordinarily wide range of haberdashery including ribbons, braids, cords, trimmings, beads, sequins, feathers, curtain tassels and tie-backs. Mail order available.
Tel: 020 7434 3899
www.vvrouleaux.com

PAINTS, VARNISHES AND SPECIAL FINISHES

APPLICRAFT
Transfer glaze (as used for floral cupboard on page 101).
Tel: 01932 872572

B&Q
Wide range of decorating paints in contemporary colours.
Tel: 020 7576 6502
www.diy.com

CROWN PAINTS
Decorating and colour advice plus order paint on-line.
Tel: 01254 704951
www.crownpaint.co.uk

DULUX
Wide range of decorating paints in a vast choice of shades.
Tel: 01753 550555
www.dulux.co.uk

HAMMERITE
Makers of specialist metallic paints and enamels.
Tel: 01661 830000
www.hammerite.com

HOMEBASE
Tel: 0870 900 8098
www.homebase.co.uk

HUMBROL
Makers of the Glass Etch spray for creating a frosted effect on glass or Perspex (as used for the etched mirror frame project on page 24 and the Perspex screen on page 114). Also makers of chrome paints (as used on the silver chair on page 91).
Tel: 01482 701191

INTERNATIONAL PAINT
Range of paints, including floor paints and multi-surface primer.
Tel: 01962 711001
www.plascon.co.uk

L. CORNELISSEN & SON
Suppliers of a wide range of traditional artists' materials plus aluminium, silver and gold leaf and specialist tools for gilding.
Tel: 020 7636 1045
www.cornelissen.co.uk

LIBERON

Gilt cream, waxes and wood finishes.
Tel: 020 7272 2446

LONDON GRAPHIC CENTRE

Specialist shop offering a range of design sundries, art and craft supplies plus a good selection of handmade papers.
Tel: 020 7759 4500
www.londongraphics.co.uk

THE PAINTED FINISH

Glazes, varnishes and tools for creating paint effects.
Tel: 01926 842376
www.craftychick.com

PÉBÉO

Craft paints for fabric, glass and porcelain.
Tel: 02380 701144
www.pebeo.com

PLASTI-KOTE

Makers of aerosol spray paints for decorative use, including glass-frosting spray, metallic finishes and sprays suitable for use with stencils.
Tel: 01223 836400
www.spraypaint.co.uk

TIRANTI

Aluminium foil (as used for metallic markers, spotted blind and metal lampshade on pages 139, 191 and 173).
Tel: 020 7636 8565 or for mail order 0118 930 2775

WOOLWORTHS

Stockists of Dylon fabric dyes (see page 210) plus a small range of glues, paint brushes and paints.
Tel: 01706 862789
www.woolworths.co.uk

STORAGE

THE COTSWOLD COMPANY
Storage furniture and baskets
in wood and woven fibres. Mail
order available.
Tel: 01252 391404
www.cotswoldco.com

HARVEY BAKER DESIGN
Wooden storage boxes and bins
(used for drilling projects on
page 55).
Tel: 01803 521515
www.harvey-baker-design.co.uk

HEAL'S
Contemporary storage
accessories.
Tel: 020 7636 1666
www.heals.co.uk

THE HOLDING COMPANY
Wide range of baskets, boxes,
chests and other more unusual
storage solutions.
Tel: 020 7610 9160
www.theholdingcompany.co.uk

IKEA
Free-standing storage units and
wall-mounted fittings in a range
of finishes, from country pine
to modern metal and glass.
Tel: 020 8208 5600 for details of
your nearest store
www.ikea.co.uk

LAKELAND LIMITED
Unusual and practical storage
solutions by mail order.
Tel: 01539 488100
www.lakelandlimited.co.uk

MCCORD DESIGN BY MAIL
Willow and wicker storage
baskets, chrome racks and rails.
Tel: 0870 908 7005
www.emcord.com

MUJI
Minimalist storage accessories
made from cardboard,
polypropylene and steel.
Tel: 020 72221 9360 for details
of your nearest store
www.muji.co.uk

BOMBAY DUCK

Decorative contemporary
accessories, including vases,
photo frames and beaded
items.
Tel: 020 8749 8001
www.bombayduck.co.uk

THE CONRAN SHOP

Contemporary accessories and
soft furnishings plus storage
items including cookware and
tableware.
Tel: 020 7591 8702
www.conran.co.uk

MARKS & SPENCER

A wide range of contemporary
and traditional accessories.
Tel: 020 7935 4422 for stockists
or 0845 603 1603 for mail order
www.marks-and-spencer.com

PRICE'S CANDLES

Wide range of decorative,
scented, traditional and garden
candles.
Tel: 01234 264 500
www.prices-candles.co.uk

SCUMBLE GOOSIE

Ready-to-paint furniture and
accessories including screens,
trays and lamp bases.
Tel: 01453 731315
www.scumble-goosie.co.uk

SHAKER

Shaker-style wooden furniture,
peg rails, oval storage boxes
and folk-art accessories.
Tel: 020 7935 9461
www.shaker.co.uk

WAX LYRICAL

Decorative candles and
candleholders.
Tel: 020 8561 0235
www.waxlyrical.co.uk

WINDOW TREATMENTS

ARTISAN
Wide range of poles and finials, from trendy to traditional in style.
Tel: 01772 203555

THE BRADLEY COLLECTION
Stylish curtain poles and finials in wood and sleek steel.
Tel: 01449 722724
www.bradleycollection.co.uk

THE CURTAIN EXCHANGE
Quality second hand curtains bought and sold.
Tel: 020 7731 8316
www.thecurtainexchange.cwc.net

ECLECTICS
Made-to-measure and ready-made roller and Roman blinds in smart modern designs.
Tel: 0870 010 2211
www.eclectics.co.uk

JOHN LEWIS
Wide range of fabrics and haberdashery plus curtain-making products.
Tel: 020 7629 7711
www.johnlewis.co.uk

MARKS & SPENCER
Curtains and blinds, poles and tiebacks.
Tel: 020 7935 4422 for stockists or 0845 603 1603 for mail order
www.marks-and-spencer.com

RUFFLETTE
Tiebacks, blind and eyelet kits and curtain-making products.
Tel: 0161 998 1811
www.rufflette.com

ARGOS
Furniture, bedlinen, lighting and accessories.
Tel: 0870 600 3030
www.argos.co.uk

Bhs
Furniture, bedlinen, lighting and lighting accessories and fittings.
Tel: 020 7262 3288 for details of your nearest store
www.bhs.co.uk

DEBENHAMS
Furniture, bedlinen, window dressings and lighting.
Tel: 020 7408 4444 for details of your nearest store
www.debenhams.co.uk

HABITAT
Contemporary accessories including mirrors, picture frames and vases.
Tel: 0845 601 0740
www.habitat.net

HEAL'S
Contemporary accessories.
Tel: 020 7636 1666
www.heals.co.uk

IKEA
Affordable furnishing fabrics and storage accessories.
Tel: 020 8208 5600
www.ikea.co.uk

JOHN LEWIS
A wide range of furniture, fabrics, wallcoverings, bedlinen, lighting and accessories.
Tel: 020 7629 7711 for details of your nearest store
www.johnlewis.co.uk

LAURA ASHLEY
Classic and country-style fabrics, soft furnishings and accessories. Mail order available.
Tel: 0870 562 2116 for stockists or 0800 868 100 for mail order
www.lauraashley.com

MARKS & SPENCER
A wide range of furniture, fabrics, window dressings, lighting, paints and accessories.
Tel: 020 7935 4422 for stockists or 0845 603 1603 for mail order
www.marks-and-spencer.com

ONE-STOP SHOPS

ONE-STOP SHOPS

MCCORD (ROOMS BY DESIGN)
Contemporary and vintage-style furniture and accessories by mail order.
Tel: 0870 908 7020
www.emccord.com

MONSOON HOME
Soft furnishings and accessories with an ethnic style.
Tel: 020 7313 3000
www.monsoon.co.uk

NEXT HOME
Contemporary furniture, accessories and bedlinen. Mail order available.
Tel: 0870 243 5435 for stockists or 0845 600 7000 for mail order
www.next.co.uk

THE PIER
Reasonably priced accessories and soft furnishings.
Tel: 0845 609 1234
www.pier.co.uk

CONTRIBUTORS

BBC Worldwide and *BBC Good Homes* magazine would like to thank the following contributors.

Jo Barnes: page 154
Juliet Bawden: pages 42, 56, 62, 64, 82, 158, 174, 186
Evelyn Bennett: page 162
Petra Boase: pages 76, 106, 176
Chloe Brown: pages 30, 128
Jane Burdon: pages 26
Jo Carmichael: page 86
Sacha Cohen: pages 122, 124, 126
Jan Dabbous: pages 66, 68, 70, 72, 146, 202
Alison Davidson: page 144
Cris Donet: page 110
Marion Elliott: pages 138, 172, 190
Mary Fitzmaurice: pages 192, 194, 196
Jane Forster: page 100
Mark Gregory: page 54
Emma Hardy: page 208

Zoe Hope: pages 32, 84
Alison Jenkins: pages 24, 104, 114, 152, 182, 204
Jayne Keeley: page 164
Tracey Kendall: page134
Andrea Maflin: page 96
Lucyina Moodie: page 78
Neeley Moore: pages 40, 80
Kitty Percy: pages 8, 10, 12, 14, 20, 22, 88, 130, 136, 166, 168, 170
Nicky Phillips: page 18
Maggie Philo: pages 46, 160
Sophie Robinson: pages148, 178, 200
Fran Soler: page 142
Wendy Uren: pages 28, 108, 206
Lynda Watts: pages 36, 52, 102
Wendy Wilson: pages 48, 132